# REMINGTON

## THE HISTORY *of* A
## BALTIMORE NEIGHBORHOOD

## KATHLEEN C. AMBROSE

THE
History
PRESS

Published by The History Press
Charleston, SC 29403
www.historypress.net

*Front cover, top:* The Ellsberry alligator/crocodile mural on the Twenty-eighth Street bridge. *Author's collection.*
*Front cover, bottom:* The Easter Parade on Charles Street. *The Palmer Collection.*
*Back cover, top:* The Davises, one of the many families that migrated to Remington from the Carolinas in the 1940s. *Courtesy of Jane Davis.*
*Back cover, bottom:* Athletic organizations encourage community cohesiveness. *Courtesy of Ken Walters.*

First published 2013

Manufactured in the United States

ISBN 978.1.62619.125.9

Library of Congress CIP data applied for.

*Notice*: The information in this book is true and complete to the best of our knowledge. It is offered without guarantee on the part of the author or The History Press. The author and The History Press disclaim all liability in connection with the use of this book.

# CONTENTS

Preface                                                                  5
Resources                                                                7
Acknowledgements                                                         9

1. Defining Remington: Early Settlers and the Mills                      11
2. Roads, Rocks and Railways:
    Development of a Blue-Collar Neighborhood                            27
3. A Neighborhood of Exits: Bridges, Churches and Schools               45
4. The Skeeter Scare of 1915:
    U.S. Marine Hospital and Community Health                            63
5. The Three Lives of Remington: Developing Diversity                   71
6. Fleeting Prosperity: A Mirror to the City                            93
7. Redefining Remington: Community Sustainability                       101

Afterword                                                                119
Selected Bibliography                                                    121
Index                                                                    123
About the Author                                                         127

# PREFACE

I bow down to those historians who have attempted to preserve Remington history before the advent of the computer age and thank them profusely for saving me the arduous task of beginning from scratch. In the dark ages before the World Wide Web, research required trips to Annapolis, the Maryland Historical Society and the Maryland Room at the Enoch Pratt Free Library. Even with today's Internet resources, interpreting land records, deeds and wills is hard work. But now we have the Web, and we have Facebook and we have a way of communicating our personal histories, however irreverent they may be. And much of Remington history *is* irreverent!

Remington does not exist because of some governmental classification or subjective boundaries; it exists because people settled here, worked here, stayed here and created a viable neighborhood. I apologize for my use of the terms "working-class" and "blue-collared," as they seem a bit derogatory in this age of political correctness, but nothing else defines the Remington people better.

Of course, there was no Remington until about 1850, when an estate owner decided to lay out an avenue and name it after himself. Then people started "passing through Remington" to travel to the north. The mayor and city council of Baltimore graciously named the neighborhood after the estate owner, William Remington, as a token of their appreciation for all the land he donated to the formation of Wyman Park. He didn't, however, even get a piece of the park named after him.

It is difficult to define Remington by geographical means. Waterways, rocky terrain and densely wooded land virtually isolated Remington, and such isolation fostered a community through its workforce. Original Remington settlers worked the quarries; they were teamsters who traveled the Falls Road Turnpike to deliver goods; they were merchants who developed industry in and around the Jones Falls waterway. There may have been a few mill workers in the group, too. The best way to define the area is socially and culturally. How did Remington develop its "notoriety" as a diverse, working-class neighborhood? It's not going to be a pretty story, but inquiring minds want to know, so let's take a magical history tour of Remington and its people to find out.

# RESOURCES

There are numerous images, maps and newspapers online that aid in the identification of the street names and places I mention within the text. The best site for Baltimore maps is at Johns Hopkins University libraries and can be found at https://jscholarship.library.jhu.edu. The Enoch Pratt Library is also a fount of information at http://www.prattlibrary.org, as well as the Baltimore County Public Libraries at http://www.bcpl.info. The Maryland Historical Society shares a portion of its images online at http://www.mdhs.org. Of course, land deeds and wills are the purview of the Maryland State Archives at http://msa.maryland.gov, and Baltimore City has its own archives at http://baltimorecityhistory.net. ProQuest has the online archives of the *Sun* and other historic newspapers that can usually be accessed through libraries and universities. One of the most important resources used in creating this publication were my neighbors.

# ACKNOWLEDGEMENTS

My eternal thanks goes to John McGrain, as a recipient of the Mayor's History Honor and author, he is a well-known molinographer whose publications and images on the subject contributed greatly to this work. Warm thanks goes to Jack Manion for his work on the Mount Royal area and quarries of the Jones Falls; his cousin, Eugene Sattler, for sharing his memories of Remington and SS Philip and James; Jim and Jane Gilpin for sharing their history; ditto for Ken Walters Jr., Christine Walters-Frize, Crystal Carter and Fay Holden. I also appreciate the contributions of Betsy Childs and Blaine Carvalho for preserving images of past historical ventures; Bonita Martin and Michael Brown for the Palmer Collection; the Greater Remington Improvement Association for providing support and sustainability for the community; and Ms. Dee Dee Clark for the SS Philip and James archival images. A thank you also goes out to Fred Rasmussen at the *Sun* for taking the time to interview me and generate interest in the project. Special thanks to the Mooney, Krout and Wilgis families and the hundreds of other neighbors who had stories to share. You *are* Remington!

CHAPTER 1

# DEFINING REMINGTON

## *Early Settlers and the Mills*

*As he navigated the steep and rocky slopes of his new plantation, Nicholas Haile contemplated the wisdom of his purchase. The stream would just barely support a mill and the rough land could never be farmed. The woods surrounding him seemed hostile and forbidding. He thought it a shame he had given the name Folly to his other estate, because the term more aptly applied to this landscape.*

## THE EARLY SETTLERS

How to define an area with such auspicious beginnings? What is now Remington was located in part of the Patapsco Lower Hundreds of Baltimore County, which contained approximately twelve thousand acres of wooded land interspersed with many streams, rivers and ponds. The Jones Falls was the dividing line between Patapsco Lower and Middlesex Hundreds and, until recently, marked the western boundary of Remington. In the early eighteenth century, the lands comprising Remington remained undeveloped and without owners. Its rocky terrain made it unusable for farming and travel, but this did not deter some speculators. On January 10, 1701, Nicholas Haile laid out one hundred acres of property he named "Haile's Addition," which straddled both sides of Stony Run, a waterway that emptied into the falls.

Nicolas was a native Virginian and a lucrative businessman who already owned hundreds of other acres in the Baltimore area, and he had just

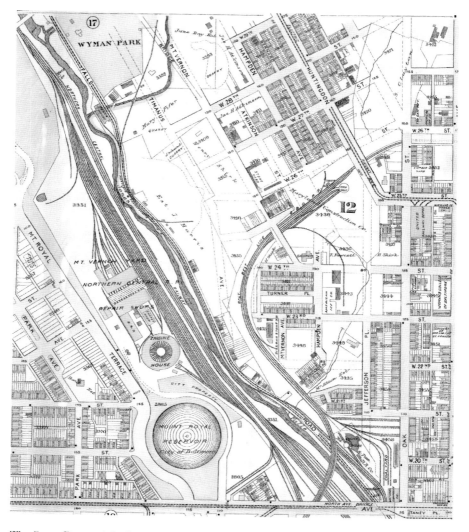

The Stony Run and the Jones Falls are emphasized on G.W. Bromley's 1906 map of Baltimore City. *Public domain.*

married into the prominent Garrett family of Virginia with hopes of acquiring more land. In addition to the "Addition," he was also one-half owner of "Merryman's Lott," 110 acres that abutted the "Addition" and would become the site of Johns Hopkins University. His vast estates covered parts of Roland Park, Wyman Park, Hampden and Remington. Haile had no problem defining his neighborhood since he owned them all. Haile and his partner in land barony, Charles Merryman, owned most of the acreage around Stony Run, from the Jones Falls to Harford Road.

Haile's marriage to Frances Garrett produced eight or nine children, and the family resided in a one-story farmhouse named Liliendale, on land that is now probably home to Levering Hall of the Johns Hopkins University Homewood Campus. Nicholas died in 1730, leaving Frances as executrix. Frances got to live in the house as long as she wanted, but Nicholas's son, Neale, inherited the house after her death and, according to his father's will, Neale also received a part of "Haile's Addition adjoining…[the] dwelling plantation…to begin at a great stone standing upon Great Run [Stony Run] of this tract and to run with a straight line to a bounded black oak." Nicholas left the other part of "Haile's Addition" to his daughter Mary, but she died soon after her father and Neale got the entire parcel. Neale hung around the farmhouse for the next seventeen years before he and his wife, Sarah, decided to move to upper Baltimore County. He sold most of his Stony Run property to Joseph Ensor in 1771, who in turn mortgaged his real estate through the ubiquitous Charles Carroll of Carrollton.

Joseph Ensor was intent on buying most of the Hampden-Woodberry area (at this point in time, Remington was considered a part of the Woodberry Mills system). His total real estate holdings in the area amounted to 1,195 acres, all of it mortgaged to Carroll for £3,191. He resided on an estate called "Seed Ticks Plenty" in Hampden until his death, sometime at the close of the Revolutionary War, and he is believed to be buried there. He had bought over one hundred acres of Merryman's Lott and thirty acres of Haile's Addition, so he was the heavily mortgaged owner of the northern part of Remington in the late eighteenth century. He married Mary Bouchelle from Cecil County, who gave birth to three children: Augustine, Mary and Joseph Jr. Augustine died young; Mary married Major Edward Oldham, of Cecil County and moved there; and Joseph Jr., the major heir, was declared insane in 1782. Elijah Merryman and David McMechen became the trustees of Junior's estate, and they purchased and then sold 1,040 acres of his property. The trustees placed an advertisement in 1784 that described the property as a "valuable estate, situated from two to four miles from Baltimore Town, part of which lies on Jones's Falls, which is laid out and divided into farms, from twenty to one hundred acres each, several of which have excellent mill seats." The farms would have been located farther north, outside of what would become Remington boundaries, and the property for sale excluded the lower seventy-acre portion of "Haile's Addition" that Ensor had declined to purchase because of its rocky terrain.

The south part of Remington was ruled by Jonathan Hanson who, in 1725, purchased 340 acres he called "Mount Royal." About one-half of the property, approximately 170 acres, covered the area from North Avenue to Twenty-ninth Street. Hanson was a Philadelphia Quaker who married Kezia Murray of Baltimore County, and they had one child, Jonathan II, before she died in 1718. Jonathan then remarried Mary Price, also of Baltimore County, who gave birth to three children, alliteratively named Mary, Margaret and Mordecai. The elder Hanson is notable for building the first mill along the Jones Falls in 1711, probably near his Fell's Point property. He was obviously not a happy camper, though, as his death in 1726 was ruled a suicide by the coroner. As a result of this "unlawful and unnatural act," all his property was forfeited to the province. His wife had to petition the court to get it all back. The younger Jonathan eventually became the manager of the Mount Royal plantation. In his will, dated December 26, 1785, Jonathan Hanson II bequeathed to his second wife, Mary, the houses, plantation and upper gristmill. His son, Amon, also inherited another mill on the property.

While all these huge estates surrounded the borders of what would become Remington, nobody actually chose to live there. The large plantation owners preferred to build their dwellings on Baltimore's pinnacles. The Hansons lived in what is now Mount Vernon and Bolton Hill; the Merrymans and Hailes chose Homewood and Guilford; and the Ensors lived in Hampden. Talk about a neighborhood with a complex! It was early days, and Baltimore was just beginning to form a populace. Even so, Remington would remain undeveloped for quite some time.

# THE MILLS

Today, standing at the approximate area where Stony Run would meet the Jones Falls, it is easy to imagine the wilderness that confronted the early developers of the area. By the late eighteenth century, mills were established on both sides of the falls. With the energy and destruction of a runaway train, the Jones Falls tore through Baltimore from the Greenspring Valley to the Inner Harbor. Merchants and millers began vying for property along its banks to harness its power and access its water, and real estate developers saw lucrative capital ventures. By the 1780s, Baltimore was bustling with new housing. Roads were cobbled, bridges were built, streets were lit and, to pay for it all, property was taxed.

As Baltimore Town grew, so did the wealth of those individuals who had invested in the undeveloped land surrounding the town. Josias Pennington had put his money into developing the mills along the Jones Falls, from east to west, and purchased the lower seventy-acre portion of "Haile's Addition" with a mill situated south of the confluence of Stony Run and the Jones Falls. During the grain boom of the 1780s, even a small mill could turn a profit for investors. (The Maryland State Archives Special Collections has two paintings of Pennington and his mill that can be viewed online.)

In 1789, Josias Pennington deeded to Charles and William Jessop a portion of the "Addition." Three years later, Elisha Tyson, George Leggett and the Jessop brothers all owned mill seats along the eastside of the falls. Four of the larger gristmills that have been identified as having property lying within the Remington area were Rock Merchant Mill, Union Mill, Mount Royal Forge and Mill and Laurell Merchant Mill. The vast acreage that was sometimes included with the purchase of the mill seats was subdivided and sold separately. As the population of the Baltimore harbor increased, this portion of North Baltimore County became a refuge for those wealthy landowners who wanted to escape the noise, pollution and disease of the wharves and warehouses (and taxes—they really wanted to escape those taxes).

The mills traded ownership with dizzying frequency. In addition to the portion of land sold to the Jessops, Pennington later sold fifty-four acres of adjoining property to Bernard Gilpin, a planter living in Montgomery County. The Jessops sold their mill seat to two millers from the Gwynn's Falls area, Samuel and Thomas Hollingsworth, and they in turn increased their acreage by purchasing a portion of the Gilpin property. The Hollingworth's Mill location is the most identifiable because of the dam that can still be viewed on the Jones Falls. On July 22, 1815, Samuel Hollingsworth placed an advertisement in the *American* for another miller to join him and his sons, but a month later, "Rock Mill," as it was named, was for sale. The mill was described as being two miles from the city, containing a fall of eighteen feet and designed using the "Oliver Evans improved plan." The mill stayed on the market for quite some time as Ann and Samuel Hollingsworth again advertised its sale on May 20, 1818. The description states that the fall was now twenty feet as the dam had been rebuilt after flooding damaged it in August 1817.

The Hollingsworth's round falls provided a picturesque setting for many local nineteenth-century artists. The Maryland Historical Society has a print entitled "Jones Falls Near Baltimore," engraved by J. Hill from a painting by

*Above*: Rock Mill, Hollingsworth Mill, Tinamus Mill—every owner gave the mill seat a new name and often a new look. *Courtesy of John McGrain.*

*Opposite, top*: Photo of the Round Falls looking north on the Jones Falls at the Hollingsworth Dam. The "new" Cedar Avenue Bridge appears in the background above it. *Courtesy of John McGrain.*

*Opposite, bottom*: The Round Falls of Hollingsworth Dam, looking south from Falls Road. *Courtesy of John McGrain.*

J. Shaw, which shows a small, low mill on the east bank below a curved dam. It depicts a millhouse four stories tall and a bridge with three arches appears in the background. The arched bridge is also found in an 1820 painting by Cornelius de Beet entitled "Hollingsworth's Mill." While both of these views show the gable end of the building pointing downstream, the mill had been obviously rebuilt by 1840, when Alfred Jacob Miller painted it. His painting depicts the gable-end perpendicular to the falls with two rows of dormer windows that had been added to the roof.

A postcard from the 1930s depicts the Hollingsworth Mill and the famous round falls. The Cedar Avenue Bridge, shown spanning the falls, was constructed in 1890 by King Iron Bridge Manufacturing of Cleveland at a cost of $30,000. Consisting of two eighty-foot spans, it rose over the Northern Central Railroad tracks, Falls Road and the Jones Falls. Using gneiss rock and granite from the local quarries as a basis for the piers, marble from Upper Baltimore County's Beaver Dam quarry was added as backing. Despite public outcry about the cost, the bridge was heavily used by residents and visitors to access Druid Hill Park. *Courtesy of John McGrain.*

The Hollingworths eventually sold the mill to Henry White in 1833. The Sidney map of 1850 notes it as the White Mill, but White had already sold the mill to the Baltimore Water Company that same year. The Rock Mill passed from the private water company to the mayor and city council in 1854, and the City later advertised it for sale in the *Sun* newspaper on January 29, 1863, calling it "surplus property." It was, however, still in operable condition as a gristmill, and several millers worked it while it was under City control. John G. Hewes eventually bought the property in 1863, and he, in turn, sold it to David Carroll in 1872.

In 1882, Carroll's daughter, Mrs. Fannie Timanus, inherited the mill and the two acres of land on which it was situated. The mill just happened to abut the property of her husband, John F. Tinamus, the father of the future mayor E. Clay Timanus.

The mill, which once ran day and night, was out of operation by 1915. The City once again took ownership for the purposes of flood control, and in 1933, the mill was razed.

This photo of Timanus Mill in 1907 was rescued from the refuse at the Maryland Academy of Sciences by Claire Richardson. The photographer is unknown, but some of the academy's photos were done by John Widgeon, noted African American curator and specimen collector. *Courtesy of John McGrain.*

Well, enough dawdling down this portion of Stony Run—let's see what's happening upstream.

While Rock Mill operated from the power of the Jones Falls and processed four hundred bushels of grist per day, Union Mill was operating one hundred feet up the hill on the northwest bank of Stony Run and was producing a mere forty bushels in the same time period. Archival information shows the mill was owned by John Baxley in 1791 and was probably in existence well before then. In 1788 advertisements appeared in local newspapers offering a mill seat on "Ensor's Run" describing a place suitable for a paper mill or sawmill among other suggestions and that, because of rock formations, needed no dam. Even though Stony Run was considered a weak stream, a mill was erected. When Bernard Gilpin became owner in 1802, he advertised it with an output of thirty thousand bushels per year with enough water power for another wheel. The mill went up for auction in April 1805, but there were no buyers. Gilpin eventually sold it to Benjamin Ellicott in 1807, who bequeathed it to Andrew Ellicott in 1837. The mill was described as being on the north side of Ensor's Run (one of the four names given to Stony Run) with a large fall of water and composed of fifty-six acres. Sometime between 1837 and 1841, the mill burnt down and the Ellicott property was advertised for sale in May 1841. James Bay bought the property, including the remnants of the mill, in 1842. This would be a good time for the Jane Bay story.

James Bay had already bought property along the Jones Falls at auction in 1832 and continued to expand his real estate through September 1848. The Bay Estate would become the largest parcel of private land in north Remington and would remain so for quite some time. Originally from Harford County, James and Jane settled in Baltimore in the 1830s, where James had purchased a portion of the Mount Royal and Stony Run properties. The Bays built a cottage along the falls for use as a summer home but maintained a residence in Mount Royal. Census records show that James was a milliner and Jane a physician, which is proof that nineteenth-century census takers were not big on accuracy. James, far from being a hat maker, was actually a landowner whose income was derived from the collection of rents and proceeds from the mill. Jane was not a physician but a "psychic," which probably raised a few eyebrows in the neighborhood. A childless couple, they fostered orphan boys in both their Mount Royal and Stony Run houses, and when James died in 1870, Jane continued both her spiritualist and foster mother roles. As a widow, she depended on her attorney, Bernard Carter, to oversee her financial affairs and properties, which were extensive, but her husband had invested well. The Swann Lake Railroad was expanding throughout the state and condemning property along the Falls Road corridor. Jane's property was confiscated as soon as James was buried. Creditors descended on the widow in droves, and she was overwhelmed with the responsibilities of property management. She placed advertisements in local newspapers to rent out her ice ponds along Stony Run, and property that the railroad hadn't confiscated was sold by auction. She sued for uncollected rents, but things were looking bleak. Jane still maintained her Mount Royal residence, but Stony Run was falling into disrepair. Throughout her financial fiasco, Jane still fostered her orphaned boys, but the pressures were too much and her physical and mental health deteriorated.

When she died in 1876, her estate was valued close to $300,000, and she left most of that to establish a home for orphaned boys on her Baltimore County land. Both eyebrows and ire were raised over this decision. Her will took close to two years to probate, with Carter overseeing the formation of the Jane Bay Home for Boys trust. The trust was supposed to accumulate interest

The Stony Run was considered a "weak stream," but it was able to support several mills along its bank. This particular mill was probably located farther upstream from Union Mill. *Courtesy of John McGrain.*

for five years before the construction of a building. While most of the heirs accepted the terms, Jane's nephew Senator Nathan Scott and his sister Jennetta protested the will, declaring Jane was mentally incapacitated at the time she dictated the terms. He used Jane's spiritualism as an example of her mental state. The contest went to court where dozens of spiritualists were called to the stand to prove that psychic abilities did not necessarily mean insanity, and the court agreed. Her will stood. While the trust was accumulating interest, none of the Bay land around Stony Run could be sold or developed in the interim. So the land sat and the mill was unusable, but there was still the stream that Jane once advertised as a perfect place for ice skating. Want to check that out?

If there was a large fall of water back then, I can't see it. As far as it being a "weak stream," it looks like it couldn't float a toy boat much less turn a mill wheel. It does, however, have a nice trail to follow. Speaking of trails, let's go back down to The Hollow (a Remington term referring to the valleys of Jones Falls and Stony Run) and walk the Jones Falls Trail that the city and state planners so graciously provided for us. Which way, north or south? I think south.

Today the Mount Royal neighborhood, which lies south of Remington, is no longer adjoining the community because of the surrounding infrastructure,

Once able to support a gristmill, today the Stony Run is a mere trickle. Its confluence with the Jones Falls ended when Falls Road was developed. *Author's collection.*

The Jones Falls Trail. The Jones Falls Trail Plan covers 4.25 miles of wooded hills and scenic views along the falls from Penn Station to Clipper Mill and an additional 2.75 miles through Druid Hill. *Author's collection.*

but property ownership in the eighteenth century had no such boundaries and often crept over district lines and waterways. The plantation named Mount Royal originally contained 340 acres of land. The Mount Royal Forge and its associated mill were built on 11 acres of this property in 1753 by the Baltimore Company. The plantation meandered over the Jones Falls' east and west banks and upstream into the county. The mill itself was pictured on the west side of the falls, just above the boundary line near the first tollgate on Falls Road, and was operated under lease by George Leggett and William Taggart. Leggett and Taggart took possession and then immediately sold the mill to neighboring landowner Dr. Solomon Birckhead in 1795. Like the other mills along the Jones Falls, it changed ownership quickly. Birckhead sold it to Thomas Rutter Jr. and John Rutter, who advertised its sale in 1804; General John Stricker owned it in 1814; Hugh Jenkins was renting it in 1822; in 1833, it became the property of John Bradford, who sold it to Stephen Goudy in 1845; and it was finally taken over by a private water company that sold it to the city in 1854. The Mount Royal Mill was damaged in a flood in 1858, and the city's water board offered this flour mill as surplus property. Whew! This is hard to imagine. Luckily, the Baltimore County Public Library's Legacy website has a black-and-white photo reproduction of a colored engraving from 1828 by Bichebois after a painting by William Guy Wall that depicts the scenario. That's right, a photo of an engraving of a painting. Today, by walking along the North Avenue Bridge, you can view the vast railway system that now runs over the mill property.

Time to get off the bridge and check out what we missed by choosing the southern route over the northern path. No surprise that we will find another mill.

Elisha Tyson—there was a guy with a history. Philanthropist, abolitionist, politician and mills owner, his Mount Vernon Mills are now a multi-use property with offices, restaurants and apartments. He was one of the mill owners authorized to develop Falls Road Turnpike. Laurell Merchant Mill, however, was not one of his successes. Even though it was processing more grist than Union Mill, it was in fearful shape. After Elisha's death, his son Nathan purchased an acre of land from the Jessops and tried to upgrade the facilities by installing a coal furnace, which resulted in a fire causing total destruction to it and the nearby Stony Works Cotton Factory. The ruins were bought by Hugh Jenkins, who believed it was still "substantial" enough to lease to textile makers William Mason, Horatio N. Gambrill and David N. Carroll (those Carrolls will keep popping up). It is thought that this mill may have eventually been incorporated into the Mount Vernon Mills complex.

*Top*: Ruins of the Laurell Merchant Mill, burned out and equipped with a chimney from a grain drier, are seen in this photo circa 1866 by David Bachrach, described in a pen inscription as looking down Jones Falls below Mount Vernon Mill. *Courtesy of John McGrain.*

*Bottom*: The Jones Falls provided a photo-op for those lucky enough to possess a camera. Florence Palmer is pictured posing below Hollingsworth Dam. Today, the picturesque backdrop has been replaced with the high cement walls of the Jones Falls Expressway. *The Palmer Collection.*

As steam replaced water as a means of power, the gristmills slowly fell into decline. Textiles replaced grain in the Hampden mills, but those within the Remington area simply folded to make way for new infrastructure.

Well, back and forth along the Jones Falls, and it's time to take a breather. Perhaps we should sit by Hollingsworth's Dam and contemplate the water.

CHAPTER 2

# ROADS, ROCKS AND RAILWAYS

*Development of a Blue-Collar Neighborhood*

*Josias Pennington stood by the run and surveyed the millworks. A wagon was traveling down the west bank of the falls toward Baltimore-town, probably from Tyson's Mill. He turned his face to the overcast sky. It looked like another summer storm was on its way and he hoped the falls would not crest onto the old, battered Indian path that ran through his property. He absently gazed toward the mill seat he had deeded to the Jessops and wondered what improvements Charles and William were contemplating. More than likely the same thing all the millwrights along the Jones Falls envisioned to ensure their prosperity: a decent road.*

## THE JONES FALLS TURNPIKE

We seem to be languishing in the Jones Falls Valley, but that's where all the action was way back then. It's hard to create a neighborhood when there's no way of getting there.

Although the Revolution left the State of Maryland bankrupt, the grain merchants and millwrights had profited. The exportation of grain became big business in the 1780s, drawing unemployed citizens from other parts of Maryland to Baltimore. The mills were prospering, but the millwrights along the Jones Falls were not happy. They wanted a good road so the farmers could easily transport their grain to the mills and their produce to the town. In 1787, three major routes had already been laid out: the Frederick, York

While industrialization along the Jones Falls brought jobs to the growing Remington community, it also brought blight, like this abandoned power plant. *Courtesy of John McGrain.*

Still standing today, this gatekeeper's house is located south of the Rockland Mill area. The tollgates were unable to pay for the necessary upkeep of the Falls Road Turnpike, and the municipal agencies took over the management. *Courtesy of John McGrain.*

and Reisterstown Turnpikes. The Jones Falls millwrights were left to their own devices. Elisha Tyson, William and Charles Jessop, John Ellicott and George Leggett petitioned the General Assembly for a permanent public road to be laid out from their mill seats to Baltimore Town. Their plans called for the road to start at Ellicott's Mill in Hampden to Tyson's Mount Vernon Mills then to the mill of the Jessops on Stony Run then to the John Baxley Mill. Baxley was somehow related to the Tysons through marriage and owned a large amount of land on the west bank of the Jones Falls as well as Union Mill on the east bank. The road would continue from Union Mill until it reached the mill of George Leggett, where it would connect with an existing road to Baltimore Town.

To develop and sustain this road, the Falls Turnpike Road Company was chartered in 1805. John Taggart and others were appointed to lay out the road beginning at North Avenue and then north as close to the falls as practicable and extending all the way to Green Spring Valley Road in upper Baltimore County.

A year later, the state legislature, at the request of the turnpike company, permitted some changes to make the route straighter and less expensive and avoid flooding. If today's Falls Road is any indication, the original planners had a different interpretation of the word "straighter." It winds through fields and around hills, crossing the falls over bridges from east to west. It climbs ridges, dips sharply into valleys and still manages to wash out in heavy rain. Farmers and merchants may have had a tough time navigating its path, but it is now one of the favorite routes for bicyclists.

The first tollgate was just north of North Avenue where the gatekeeper resided. George W. Davis was the first gatekeeper until 1845, when he was replaced by Edward Lynch. In the fall of 1846, Mr. Lynch was authorized to employ some men and have repairs made to the turnpike between the tollgate and the city because people were not happy with the condition of that portion of the road. The gatekeeper position had a large turnover rate, with Edward Lynch being replaced by William Lynch, Thomas Cooper and then, in 1870, by James Stewart, an Irishman who could handle the rigors of the position. He continued as gatekeeper until 1890.

In 1865, Henry Mankin, then a member of the company's board of managers, took charge of the operational affairs, and the following year he was elected president. He resolved to improve the conditions of the road and stated that his predecessor had found it impossible to give the turnpike the attention it needed based on his budget. The road's condition was deplorable, and a flood could easily wipe away the old and fragile bridges. Unfortunately,

This 1905 photo shows a much-polluted Jones Falls flowing in front of Penn Station on Charles Street. As early as 1817, city planners were devising methods of diverting and covering this waterway. *Author's collection.*

the company had little if any money to rectify these conditions. Investors had been distributed shares in the company, but dividends were few and far between as the debts kept mounting. Mr. Mankin proposed to build up a reserve fund of $500 for improvements. By 1867, he had succeeded in erasing past debt and had accumulated most of the reserve he had proposed. The road conditions were so much improved that the Mount Vernon Mills had donated a horse and cart to help with the transportation of materials. Remington property owners joined in the efforts to help repair the part of the turnpike through their area. Things were looking up for awhile, but then the 1867 flood washed out the road in many places and damaged or carried away several bridges. Temporary repairs were started, but a bigger flood occurred in 1868 and the damage on the road was immense. Every bridge on the road was washed away. Mankin's tenure as company president was also washed away as he was not reelected to serve in any capacity. He severed all ties, fled from the entire venture and went into the real estate business.

The southern portion of the turnpike that lay within the city boundary was ceded to the City of Baltimore in 1885. After the city boundary moved north to Cold Spring Lane, a Baltimore grand jury indicted the company for not properly maintaining that portion of the turnpike and sued to compel the company to put the road in good order. By this time, the company was bankrupt and handed over control to the city. So much for Pennington's dream of a decent road. Whatever made the planners believe laying out a road next to that monster—the Jones Falls—would succeed?

# THE QUARRIES

Rocks. Lots and lots of rocks. While the Remington millwrights were developing their properties, the Remington quarrymen were developing Baltimore. The Falls Road planners believed that the wagons from the mills and quarries would not only pay for the road through the collection of tolls, but the weight of their wide-wheeled wagons would also help keep the road in repair. Maintenance costs would be kept low because of the abundance of stone right there that could be hauled short distances. Well, we see that didn't work as well as expected, but the quarry wagons were moving along the road constantly as Baltimore was rapidly building offices and residences for its government and growing population.

Quarries were in existence on both sides of the falls about the same time as the mills were developing in the 1700s. The Mount Royal Mill had a quarry on Falls Road above North Avenue that was considered so lucrative that Leggett and Taggert didn't want to include it in the mill's sale to Dr. Birckhead. There were several quarries in operation from North Avenue to the Stony Run. The individuals who owned and operated the pits produced an enormous amount of stone for the building of Baltimore, supplying material for thousands of foundations, walls and steps. The valley was the domain of the workingman and the big rigs of horse-drawn wagons. Quarry owners, like the mill merchants, were a diversified group of businessmen who were the movers and shakers of Baltimore. They were real estate developers who sat on the boards of banking institutions; they were corporate directors who issued capital stock to other wealthy landowners; and they were employers of a large workforce that settled in Remington. They, of course, deigned to live elsewhere.

During the second half of the nineteenth century, there were a number of landowners who quarried the Jones Falls area. John Harris owned the largest quarry along Falls Road near North Avenue. Isaac H. Peddicord,

John Curley, Jacob Fifer, John G. Schwind, Thomas Gatch and James H. Atkinson were other Jones Falls quarry notables. I guess you could call them "rock" stars! Or maybe not. Shall we see?

Isaac Harrison Peddicord started as a young man in the hauling business with one small wagon and one horse. As the city grew, so did his company, and he added quarrying to his hauling and transport business. The stone quarries he acquired were on Falls Road and near the Edmondson Avenue bridge in Catonsville where he lived (I know, still not a Remingtonian). His administrative offices were on Guilford Avenue, and his stables were at 879 Greenmount Avenue, so he had to travel from one side of the city to the other on a daily basis. His Guilford offices were burned during the Great Fire of 1904, but, fortunately, the blaze spared the stable, for there would have been pandemonium if the one hundred powerful horses he owned had been crazed by the fire. Shortly after the fire, both the office and the stables were moved to 2 Saratoga Street. Business boomed because of the intensive rebuilding after the Great Fire.

The company had Baltimore's only Samson wagon, so-named for its ability to withstand the weight of the heaviest material hauled. Erecting the load was just as much of the job as hauling it, and special equipment was ordered from Pittsburg and installed on many of his sites. These loads included all the original pillars for the courthouse, a large statue for the entrance to Fort McHenry, huge sections of sewer pipe, the flagpole of Saint Agnes Hospital, the machinery in the Pratt Street powerhouse, many rooftop boilers for some of Baltimore's oldest schools and all the city water pipe until about 1932.

The most prolific business Peddicord engaged in was the quarrying. His Falls Road quarry, located between North Avenue and Twenty-third Street, produced the famous gneiss rock of the Jones Falls Valley, which was most extensively used as foundation work and in construction where rough, unfinished stone needed to be used. The stone was transported by horse and wagon, and Peddicord had two grooms, who we only know as Old Sam and Jim, to prepare the complicated hitching required for these heavy hauls. Peddicord lore tells of one typical Baltimore summer when one of the horses was overcome in the street by the heat, and Old Sam and Jim fed him beer and put ice on his head. I wonder if horses could get fined for drunk driving?

One of the Remington myths that arose from Peddicord's involvement in the rebuilding of the city after the Great Fire is that most of the debris from the conflagration was dumped in Remington and houses were built on top of it. In reality, some debris was deposited into an abandoned portion of Atkinson's quarry, where there is no residential property. A lot of debris was deposited in another abandoned quarry on the Bay Estate, and there was only one structure built on top of that. However, given how many times the city used abandoned Remington quarries as dumping grounds, I can see where the myth originated!

Since the stone yard of Hugh Sisson, the renowned Marble King of Baltimore, is close by, we should stop and wave hello. Oops, I forgot he never lived here. In fact, none of the owners of the big quarries lived in Remington, except for James H. Atkinson, who lived on Hampden Avenue, next to his quarry. Atkinson later moved to the 500 block of West Twenty-ninth Street, which is now owned by Potts & Callahan, a company that continued the heavy equipment business Peddicord initiated. Atkinson at least got a street named for him!

The Schwind quarry covered six acres located in the Twenty-eighth and Falls Road area, and it was a hotbed of activity. John G. Schwind purchased the site in 1900, but the quarry itself had a long history. Jacob Fifer owned the rocks in the mid-1840s, and he partnered with John Curley in the 1860s. Their business grew substantially. The 1880s was an era of growth for Baltimore City, with huge buildings being erected throughout its environs. Cobblestone streets were being paved, and crushed stone was in big demand. Bidding on street paving among the quarry owners was competitive, to say the least, as bribes were exchanged with street commissioners and influential politicos. When John G. Schwind took over the Fifer-Curley operation, he refused to participate in such amoral business activities—or so he told the judges. He came from a long line of quarrymen and probably had more quarries in and around Baltimore than any other owner. He organized and served for many years as president of the Baltimore Quarry Company, which was often investigated for fixing contracts with the City. Schwind, tired of the investigations and the expense of maintaining depleted quarry property, finally left the business to pursue—you guessed it—real estate development. He devoted his attention to building small dwellings throughout the south and central Remington areas. But let's go back to that hotbed of activity!

The economy was sunny in the early part of the 1880s, and Schwind constantly advertised for labor to work his Jones Falls venture. Teamsters, drivers, stonecutters, quarrymen and laborers arrived in droves and settled in south Remington area. Then came the economic Panic of 1893, and Baltimore, along with the rest of the nation, fell into a depression. Businesses closed or slowed down, causing a high rate of unemployment among the unskilled labor class. The Central Relief Committee of Baltimore began an effort to put people back to work by opening stone yards around the city for unemployed laborers to earn enough money to feed their families.

Hundreds of laborers were put to work breaking and cutting stone that would be used for municipal projects in Baltimore. One of the temporary stone yards was set up at Atkinson's quarry on Falls Road. While this relief effort provided help for some, it only increased the anger and frustration of "career" stonecutters who now had to compete with hundreds of laborers for their jobs.

Until the railroads invaded Remington, the stone quarries contributed more to the development of its social and cultural environment than the mills. The work was much more labor intensive and the workforce much more diversified. Quarries, unlike the mills, employed a debatably free black population. I say "debatably" because the Penningtons and Jessops, among others, were slaveholders. The abolitionist influences of the Tysons and Ellicotts may have dissuaded other area mill owners from utilizing slave labor, but it is unclear if the quarry owners had similar qualms. Free or slave, black men comprised a large percentage of the quarries' workforces, and these workers would eventually settle in Remington—those that lived. Most deaths in the quarries were black men who were common laborers.

The workers in the quarries were divided into two types: laborers, who broke away large rocks into smaller ones using explosives and hand tools, and stone masons, who refined the rock into building stones. The laboring jobs usually went to unskilled immigrants and black men. When they gained more experience, they could advance to stonecutting. The stonecutters or stonemasons were able to get work in stone yards around the city that specialized in preparing certain types of stone. The 1893 recession, however, was causing trouble. There were fights and other acts of violence between the quarry laborers and the relief workers. It was not unheard of for a gang from one group of laborers to cause bodily harm to keep members of another group from getting work. Italian immigrants were pouring into the harbor almost daily, and they, too, sought work in the quarries' unskilled labor market, so competition was getting fierce. Work slowdown caused many workers to seek other employment or find work in other locations and stone yards. There were periods of unemployment when the stonecutters were not able to find any job and spent a lot of time in saloons, gaining them the reputation of drunks and rowdies. In their defense, however, these guys were working with falling boulders and dynamite. The relief workers, many of whom had never pursued an outdoor career, were not used to this type of work environment and suffered countless injuries. Limbs and lives were lost on an almost daily basis, and it wasn't only the workers who suffered. The employees lived right next door to explosives and avalanches, so their lives were in peril even when they weren't working. They were the real Remingtonians, so let's see who they are.

John Mooney is my personal favorite quarryman. He and his wife, Agnes, had emigrated from Ireland to Connecticut and made their way to Baltimore in the 1870s to search for employment. He went to work in Atkinson's quarry, and the family set up house on Falls Road. On January 5, 1898, the family thought an earthquake was taking place. All the windowpanes in the house were blown away, frightening the seven Mooney children to tears. Other neighbors came running outside to check the damages to their own homes. The loud report, rumbling noise and breaking of windowpanes led many to believe that there had been an earthquake, and their fears were not allayed until the fact of the explosion became generally known: three hundred pounds of dynamite had exploded at the stone yard. The Northern Central Railroad Company was engaged in enlarging the rail yards, which included the removal of tons of rock imbedded in the hillside above the company shops. The dynamite was used for blasting the rock and was kept in a box. Every morning, three to four hundred pounds of the explosive was put into the box to be kept warm until used, but something went awry that day and the box caught fire. Flying stone wreaked havoc on windowpanes as far away as Bolton Hill, but there were only two serious injuries at the quarry and no fatalities.

The Mooney home was not the only one damaged. The Justice family also suffered destruction, and James Justice lived even closer to the explosion. He had thirty-one windowpanes blown out, as well as lost part of a partition wall; Charles and Nelson Justice lost most of the windows in their houses, too. Both the Mooneys and the Justices decided that perhaps it would be better to live a little farther away from explosives and moved "up the hill."

Mount Royal Hill, today known as Huntingdon Avenue, was the destination of many of the quarry workers and tradesmen. The Mooney and Justice families lived there for generations. The Mooneys can still be found inhabiting this part of Remington, and the stories they can tell!

Quarries had a limited life expectancy because when the quality stone ran out, the business was abandoned. Their operations had given liveliness to the Jones Falls Valley that has only now begun to return. Abandoned quarries had stories of their own, though. They filled with runoff from the roads and flooding and became illegal swimming holes and ice rinks; they housed abandoned equipment and large boulders to become refuges for fugitives and the homeless; and they became dump sites as the city's waste grew with its population. Newspaper articles were prolific as the quarries offered their tales of woe. Children playing around or swimming in the water-filled pits often

As the Jones Falls Valley developed, many of the workers' houses were either condemned to make way for the expansion of the railways or destroyed by flooding. *Courtesy of John McGrain.*

drowned. Bodies of despondent and/or intoxicated adults were frequently found floating. Sometimes, though, the news wasn't all bad. In 1931, four members of a nudist "cult" decided to relieve themselves from the heat of the typical Baltimore summer by indulging in heavy drinking and swimming in the abandoned Atkinson quarry. Neighbors called the police, who arrived in the early evening to discover the four celebrants having a rousing good time. The swimmers invited the policemen to join the fun, but the stern coppers ordered them out of the pool and into their clothes so they could enjoy a cool ride in the paddy wagon. They were charged with disorderly conduct and placed in Northern District cells to sober up. Barely had the four been settled when a call came to the station to report yet another drunken nudist sporting around the pool. The police returned to find Frank Riley doing a backstroke and wearing nothing but a rosy smile. Mr. Riley was a problem, however, as he discovered, upon leaving the water, that he had no clothes. He was taken to the station on a stretcher and covered with a blanket. He was also charged and jailed, without blanket, to await his hearing the next day. It is not

The Mooney brothers (left, center) hold court with a friend on the stoop. Neighbors gathered intermittently to say hello and catch up on the neighborhood news of the day. *Author's collection.*

known whether he was clothed when he appeared before the judge. Two of the original four were fined five dollars, and the other two asserted that they were just trying to rescue their friends from the water. Even though the police testified that none of the four appeared to desire rescuing, the judge decided that two out of four was good enough to teach a lesson. No report was given as to the court's decision regarding Mr. Riley.

The quarry pools were also a training camp for Remington youth to learn how to swim. Robert S. Krout started swimming in Atkinson's quarry when he was a mere five years old. He and several friends built a raft and floated to the middle of the pool to cool off. None of them could swim, but they quickly learned when James Atkinson pointed a rifle at them and ordered them out. Robert jumped off the raft and made it to shore in record time. Realizing that he had actually been swimming thrilled the little boy, and he spent the rest of the summer paddling around the Jones Falls pools. He perfected his body float and was able to "stomach float," where his hands, head and feet were out of the water. His performance drew crowds who were unable to discern how he managed the feat. He became a lifeguard and started teaching children how to swim. As an adult, he became a machinist, married and raised a family in his 2847 Huntingdon Avenue house. After retirement, he still swam and taught every day, performing his floating magic for Remington youth.

The Krouts, like the Mooneys, are still a big part of the Remington community. We can walk over to Twenty-seventh and Hampden Avenue right now to see Charles "Buzz" Krout and the Mooney brothers stoop sitting on the corner surrounded by a cadre of neighbors exchanging the news of the day. Say hi!

# RAILROADS

Where the quarries receded along the Jones Falls, the railroads took over. Being "railroaded" in Baltimore was not a nice process. Properties would be condemned to allow expansion of the rail system; homes would be lost with or without remuneration. Part of the Bays' estate went for the development of what would be called the Northern Central Railroad (NCRR), constructed in the 1830s. I am not going to insult my friends at the Baltimore Streetcar Museum by even trying to explain this railway system as they are currently occupying the grounds of the old NCRR station and have a plethora of information on its history. Every keen Remingtonian, however, has some knowledge of the system that ran along Stony Run: the Maryland and Pennsylvania Railroad (affectionately known as the "Ma & Pa").

The system began at the gorgeous Lehigh Station on North Avenue, where passengers had to climb down to the tracks on a set of precarious stairs. The tracks ran along the east side of the Jones Falls valley through the heart of Baltimore City. The Western Maryland and Pennsylvania Railroads also ran through the valley on the west side of the falls. The Baltimore and Ohio line grabbed some property, and its route ran through tunnels under Twenty-sixth Street and over the top of the Ma & Pa. It was one very busy, very polluted valley. No wonder the Mooneys fled uphill!

*Opposite, top*: Horses were the major means of transportation for moving baggage from the North Avenue depot. The Baltimore Streetcar Museum now occupies this site. *Courtesy of BSM.*

*Opposite, bottom*: Looking south on Falls Road, the railway contributed to the industrialization of south Remington, as evidenced by this NCRR roundhouse. *Courtesy of BSM.*

Razed in 1937 to make way for the Howard Street bridge, this photo depicts the Baltimore and Lehigh Railroad station stop at North Avenue and Howard Street at the southern boundary of Remington. It was the predecessor of the Maryland and Pennsylvania Railroad (better known as the "Ma & Pa" Railroad). The station was designed by E. Frances Baldwin. *BCPL/LW.*

Looking north from the Twenty-eighth Street bridge, this panoramic view juxtaposes the industrial freight yards with the bucolic surroundings. *Courtesy of BSM.*

The advantages of the rail system outweighed any environmental concern (not that there was that much concern for the environment in the mid-nineteenth century). Baltimore was booming, and the rails made the rich richer as well as provided jobs for the labor force. It also increased Remington's population as rail workers poured into the valley. Rapid transportation fever spread throughout the city with horse-drawn streetcars running almost constantly on Remington Avenue in the late 1850s. The first electric railway ran through the neighborhood in the 1880s. By the 1890s, there were three separate lines of streetcars running through Remington. Let's walk down Remington Avenue to see if we can find any tracks. Watch your step!

If we turn west at Twenty-seventh Street off of Remington Avenue and walk to Sisson Street, we can stand on the bridge to watch the CSX rushing through on the old B&O route, then it's off we go to Good Husbands' Row. Well, not really, because this fantastic-sounding little enclave no longer exists, but it certainly isn't forgotten. The street branched off of Hampden Avenue a little south of Twenty-third Street, and its official name was Glen Edwards Avenue. About two hundred or more persons dwelt in its thirty-some houses, which were developed about 1879. Rather than being labeled by street number, the tiny row houses were first designated by letters—A, B, C, etc.—and it was then known as ABC Row. Then people began calling it Precipice Place because of its location at the bottom of a steep hill in a deeply sloped gully. Finally, it was commonly referred to as Good Husbands' Row because, according to Remington folklore, husbands who worked in Peddicord's or Schwinn's stone quarries were unable to work when the weather got cold and snowy, so the men kept house and the women went to work, usually in the Jones Falls Valley mills.

Good Husbands' Row was bounded on the north by a rock-filled gully, on the south by a rugged wall of gneiss rock, on the east by a concrete bridge and on the west by a twisting, steep-pitched bit of cobbled road that linked it to Hampden Avenue. Hard rains swept in floods down the low-lying lane, and the summer heat was merciless because of its location behind the rock wall and gully bank. An arch over the west end of the avenue carried the B&O trains, spilling their noise and pollution onto the tiny houses. The arch did, however, provide a cool place to congregate on hot summer days.

Despite its fanciful name, Good Husbands' Row was at times Good Husbands' Woe. A seemingly large number of the wives were assaulted or committed suicide, which could probably be attributed to the proximity of Hoffman's Brewery on Twenty-third Street. In 1898, John Medinger of 408

"Good Husbands' Row" was the nickname for Glen Edwards Avenue in south Remington. Over two hundred persons inhabited its thirty-odd homes. The street was laid out in 1879 by W.H. Shipley. The properties were sold to the city in 1923 and purchased by the Baltimore Gas and Electric Company several years later. Glen Edwards was evacuated at some point in the late 1930s and used as a public dump until the 1950s. *BCPL/LW.*

Located at the end of Glen Edwards Avenue, south of the NCRR freight house, neither this watchman station nor the avenue exist today. *Courtesy of BSM.*

Glen Edwards, stabbed his wife three times with a chisel because she asked him to carry an armload of wood into the house. He later committed suicide in his padded jail cell. In 1907, Mary Mullan, of 404 Glen Edwards, drank acid in front of her daughter while her husband was out of the house. John Battila, following Medinger's example, attacked his wife with a hatchet in 1912 at their 409 Glen Edwards home. He attempted suicide by slitting his throat but managed to survive. If a wife wasn't available for uxoricide, the men turned on each other. Giovanni Rannali was killed by Ceile Yafette in a duel outside number 406 in 1911. Yafette was acquitted; what's a little roughhousing among neighbors, right?

Because of its proximity to the railroads, the residents of Good Husbands' Row also suffered train-related injuries, some fatal. Children were the most susceptible to these types of fatalities. Perhaps in an act of mercy, the entirety of Glen Edwards Avenue and all the houses on it were sold off to the City of Baltimore in 1923 and then to Consolidated (Baltimore) Gas & Electric several years later. The deed to the utility company specified that any streets that happened to be within the land parcel would be closed. It seems that all homes on Glen Edwards were razed at some point in the late 1930s, and the land was later used as a public dump until the 1950s, when it was filled in the rest of the way and became part of a salvage yard. By this time, Good Husbands' Row was just a memory to most residents, and some of those residents' memories were happy ones. South Remington youth found the salvage yard the perfect place to play, unaware of the ghosts of Glen Edwards. The only evidence of its existence today is a little glimpse of the buried arched railroad bridge behind the watchman's station on Falls Road.

# CHAPTER 3

# A NEIGHBORHOOD OF EXITS

## Bridges, Churches and Schools

*Henry Shirk looked as smug as he felt. When he had purchased fifty acres of land between Charles Street and the Jones' Falls back in 1850 for $360 an acre, he was the laughingstock of the Baltimore real estate world. It did seem for years that his prospect would never gain in value. There was simply no way to get to the property. He had tried building bridges over the Jones Falls, but they kept getting washed away by floods. Now that the City was taking interest in expanding its boundaries, the property was valuable. He looked at the purchase offer in his hand and quickly signed his name. It seemed $45,000 per acre was a very reasonable profit.*

## TWENTY-NINTH STREET BRIDGE

So where are we on our magical history tour? Oh, that's right, on Sisson Street Bridge. Between the waterways and the railroads, we can't walk too far without crossing over a bridge. Standing here looking east, we can see the Huntingdon Avenue Bridge, and if we trek over to Huntingdon (via Twenty-seventh Street), we can stand on that bridge to view the little Howard Street Bridge. On that bridge we can look south to see the big Howard Street Bridge. In 1947, city engineer William L. Chilcote averred that Baltimore had more bridges than any other city in America. Out of the 224 bridges throughout the city, 33 spanned the Jones Falls and Stony Run. About half of the bridges were maintained by the railroads.

All these little community bridges were formed by the tunneling of the B&O and the circumnavigation of the falls and supported by our nice gneiss rocks. They connected the community. Other bridges, however, were made to connect to other communities. We must see where they lead!

Walking north on Sisson Street (which used to be called Mount Vernon Avenue), we come to the Twenty-eighth Street Bridge, and we avert our eyes. This is a relatively modern construction from the 1960s that was part of the development of the Jones Falls Expressway. It's really ugly, but it connects commuters from the expressway to their homes, and the traffic is horrendous. In an effort to welcome travelers to our neighborhood, John Ellsberry designed and painted a huge mural of a series of crocodiles along its south wall for an art project in the 1980s (see back cover). Under the supervision of Mr. Ellsberry, the mural has been maintained by a number of local artists since then, for which we are eternally grateful, as the mural is the bridge's only positive aspect. Let's move on to something more architecturally pleasing.

Designed by J.E. Greiner Company, the Twenty-ninth Street Bridge is a majestic structure built in late 1937 under a New Deal public works program. Our own Potts & Callahan helped build the viaduct. Originally, the four lanes were composed of red brick with inlays of yellow brick. It crossed the Jones Falls, the valley and the railroad tracks in two strides, and at the time, it had the biggest arches ever built on the East Coast with a span of 232 feet. If we were standing beneath it, we would discover that, in addition to the inevitable reinforced concrete, it is composed of the gneiss rock from our local quarries. Maybe we'll stroll over it at another time and go to the Maryland Zoo!

When the bridge opened on December 4, 1937, plans for a formal and elegant inauguration went awry. Hundreds of unchaperoned Remington children turned the event into a carnival. Police endeavored to keep the youngsters at bay, but Remington youth prevailed. The planned parade ended up a haphazard procession, with the children running in front of Mayor Jackson and the bands. They ran back and forth from Druid Hill to Twenty-ninth Street, disrupting much of the ceremony. In addition, cars on both sides of the bridge, which the police were holding back, were revving to go. Regardless of the chaos, a fun time was had by all.

# THE HUNTINGDON AVENUE VIADUCT

Early in the morning on August 10, 1885, an electric streetcar left a barn at Howard and Twenty-fifth Streets for its first run through Remington to its terminus in Hampden. The Baltimore Passenger Railway saw a glorious future with this new service, but its stockholders did not. Where the BPR failed, however, Union Electric Railway Company succeeded by its building of the Huntingdon Avenue Bridge. Finished in 1887, the bridge spanned Stony Run and the Ma & Pa Railroad from Huntingdon Avenue to Thirty-third Street and ran two streetcar lines for more than fifty years.

The cars had woven straw seats with reversible backs, and the straw became rough and scratchy as it aged. There were a lot of women who left the cars with more snags in their stockings than when they first got on. The company paid for a lot of hosiery before it decided to switch to plush seats.

Supplying a shortcut from Remington to Hampden, the Huntingdon Avenue Bridge passed over the Maryland and Pennsylvania Railroad. Neither the bridge above nor the railroad below exist today, but stones from the trestles can be found throughout Wyman Park. *Courtesy of BSM.*

The bridge was built for trolley use only and ran two lines, the Nos. 10 and 25. It also had an eighteen-inch catwalk on each side of the tracks, and pedestrians started using the bridge as a shortcut. The company removed sections of the catwalks to discourage pedestrian use, and the poor neighborhood people tore up the rest to use as firewood. The bridge squeaked and swayed as the streetcars traveled over it, and it began to sag in its later years. It also provided great amusement to the Remington residents.

Cars were constantly driving out onto the rails by mistake, and it was a common sight to see a streetcar come sweeping down Huntingdon Avenue with a car following behind. When the trolley continued onto the bridge, the drivers kept following. The car owners would then get stuck on the rails and crossties, unable to move forward or backward. Workmen had to lay planks over the ties to get the car off the tracks. More often than not the call went out for "Big Bill," a tow truck that one shrewd Remingtonian had invested in when he saw a profit to be made.

The bridge was torn down in 1949 and the trolley rerouted along Cedar, Remington and Huntingdon Avenues. There are still some remnants of the abutments at the end of Huntingdon Avenue and along Stony Run. After our magical history tour, let's go visit the Baltimore Streetcar Museum to look at all the memorabilia it has collected about the Union Electric Railway Company and ride a streetcar!

## THE CEDAR AVENUE BRIDGE

Oh my, what has the city done to our bridge? Where is the beautiful arch truss that was depicted in so many postcards and photos? This is why we can't have nice things! Let's go back to 1890 when modernization had a sense of style.

Cedar Avenue (now Keswick Avenue) ran from University Parkway (then Merryman's Lane) through Jane Bay's property to Falls Road at the Mount Vernon Mills. It opened up the possibility of an alternative route by bridging the Jones Falls. The bridge was planned before Remington became part of the city, so the commission of Baltimore County had already made a start toward bridging the valley and built the foundation of the abutment. The structure intended by them was to have been a plain and cheap one. After annexation, city engineer Charles H. Latrobe became interested in the proposed improvements, and the enterprise was advanced to include a substantial and ornamental iron bridge supported by massive masonry piers and abutments.

The bridge was built by the King Iron Bridge Manufacturing Company of Cleveland and cost about $30,000. What a steal! It had two girders spanning nearly eighty feet over Falls Road and, of course, the railroad tracks. The two piers were huge blocks of granite weighing between six thousand to fifteen thousand pounds, and they rested on a solid foundation of gneiss rock.

Remingtonians were not used to so many escape routes and were suspicious of people from other neighborhoods coming into the area. Men and boys began forming gangs to protect "their side" of the bridges. In 1907, twelve-year-old Ivy Kaulp was shot when returning with her friends from a stroll in Druid Hill Park and walked into the middle of a gang fight on this bridge. The little girl survived, but the notoriety of the "Remington Squad," as the gang was named, was beginning to grow, despite the fact that all but one of the perpetrators lived in another neighborhood, Stone Hill. Let's hope someone can straighten out all these misguided youths!

Rust began to erode the Victorian marvel, and plans were being considered by Baltimore City to replace the structure. As a traffic artery, the two-lane bridge became obsolete when everyone got cars. The Twenty-ninth Street Bridge had taken some of the pressure off its traffic use, but every so often the old bridge would become so decrepit that cars would be banned until repairs could be made. City consultants decided the old structure had to be redecked. In 1976, neighborhood preservationists were outraged by its proposed demolition. The city had decided to tear down the historic bridge and build a new one without consulting its Commission for Historical Architectural Preservation (CHAPS), the Second District City Council delegation or the public in general. Remington residents wanted it closed to traffic and converted to a pedestrian walkway/bikeway, but the city considered their protests selfish. The city replaced the beautiful brick and stone throughway with a rather mundane steel-frame bridge that would carry traffic into Druid Hill Park. It opened in April 1978 with little fanfare and closed again less than ten years later because no one anticipated that the Jones Falls Expressway would be widened. Today, however, the bridge is part of the Jones Falls Trail, and we do finally have a pedestrian walkway/bikeway that everyone enjoys.

# THE REMINGTON AVENUE BRIDGE

Welcome to my personal bridge. Well, not really, but I know how some of those young ruffians felt guarding their turf. This is where Remington Avenue turns into Thirty-third Street, and the area miraculously becomes Wyman Park. Still looks like Remington to me! But I digress. Residents north of this bridge (Wyman Parkers) refer to it as the "Thirty-third Street Bridge," while those south of the overpass call it by its proper name: Remington Avenue Bridge. The Ma & Pa Railroad ran underneath, approximately fifty feet from the road surface. The steep grade and sharp curve had many "flivvers" flipping over the embankment and landing on the tracks below, and the trolley drivers really hated this portion of their route. Standing on top of the bridge, we can see the Stony Run Trail, which follows the path of the old Ma & Pa. The Stony Run trickles beside the trail, and huge boulders allow hikers and dog walkers the opportunity to sit by the water and take in the scenery. Let's do that for a moment of respite; we don't have to worry about being crushed under any errant autos as the old wrought-iron sides of the bridge were replaced in 1986 with reinforced concrete. If you want to see how it looked in the old days, the Maryland Historical Society has an image online at http://www.mdhs.org/digitalimage/remington-avenue-bridge-north-wyman-park-drive. Go on, pull out your tablets and check it out!

# THE GUARDIAN ANGEL

Well, we avoided meeting any Remington hoodlums protecting their side of the bridge, and do you want to know why? The Reverend George Kromer, that's why.

*Opposite, top*: Located at Remington and Thirtieth, these row houses are behind what used to be the first Guardian Angel Church. The houses were built before 1900, making them some of the oldest in north Remington. Charm City Cakes now operates from the old church site. *Author's collection.*

*Opposite, bottom*: Standing in front of the newly constructed parish hall, Father Kromer's students display decorum instilled in them by the Episcopal parish priest in this 1925 photo. *Courtesy of Betsy Childs.*

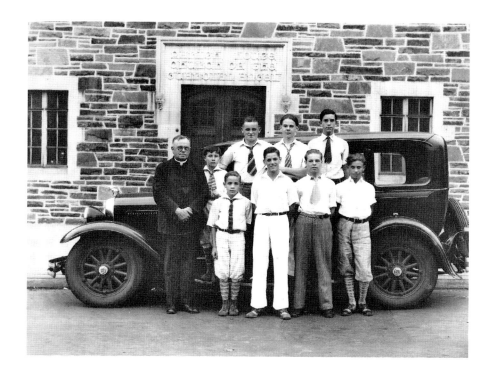

Neighborhood ruffians had greeted the thirty-two-year-old George Kromer on an autumn day in 1899 as he walked to the Guardian Angel Church on Remington and Thirtieth. "You won't last long," one young ruffian yelled. "We'll get rid of you in a hurry, the same as we did with the other preachers!" Deacon George went about his business. He had made a promise that he would go anyplace God wanted him to go and stay there as long as he was needed. That turned out to be over fifty years in Remington, something he had not foreseen.

The odds seemed against him at first. Three clergymen had preceded him at the chapel, and none lasted more than six months. There were only thirty members in the congregation, the weekly offerings averaged fifty cents, the chapel itself was little more than a wooden shed and religious apathy pervaded the entire Remington neighborhood, but Reverend Kromer was up to the challenge. He decided that social change would be more effective than a liturgical change and adopted firm order in his ministry. For example, if a member of his precious congregation failed to show up for service, he would hammer his fist on their front door early Monday morning under the pretext of checking on their health. Upon finding the congregant well, the reverend would loudly demand an explanation for their absence on Sunday. If he believed a young girl was "straying," he would visit her parents to tell them their daughter was no good and ask them what they were going to do about it. To announce the start of school each day, he would parade through the Remington streets close to the chapel, beating time on a drum slung from his shoulders and lead the children to the parish hall, Pied Piper fashion. The reverend was taking no prisoners!

His demeanor softened slightly when he married Dora Babbitt in 1901, who helped him in his ministry. The Kromers organized weekly boys' and girls' clubs that met in the basement of their Huntingdon Avenue house. Initially, fights and thefts were common during the meetings. One time Reverend Kromer was hit in the face with a bundle of newspapers and had his glasses broken, and once someone shot a brass cannon in the house. The Kromers had their hands full, but they were determined to win the errant youths' respect, and eventually they did.

His congregation grew so large that he began a fundraising campaign for a new chapel. A new chapel was built on Twenty-seventh and Huntingdon and dedicated in 1904. A parish hall was completed in the 1920s, aided by Kromer and one of his parishioners. The hall was the home of a daycare facility that was opened from 1924 to the start of World War II.

Today the Church of the Guardian Angel still carries on the Kromer tradition of social responsibility with its many programs and events that benefit the Remington children.

## SS PHILIP AND JAMES ACADEMY

For those parents looking for a more papist education for their offspring, they turned to the Saints Philip and James Catholic Church, slightly outside the Remington boundaries. The church first opened on the corner of Charles and Twenty-seventh and was designed by John Stack, a prominent Baltimore architect. It was dedicated on May 1, 1898, and was immediately under a heavy debt of mortgage from the construction costs. The congregation was relatively small, but you must remember that this part of Baltimore City was still being developed. Remington was already established along Twenty-fifth Street and Huntingdon and Remington Avenues, so most of the first congregants were the families of the Italian and Irish railroad workers and quarrymen who had limited financial resources. Needless to say, the offerings were meager.

In 1898, a school was attempted by the Sisters of Mercy from Mount St. Agnes on a property next to the church, but enrollment was dismal and the sisters withdrew from the project. A second attempt at starting a school began in 1906 under the direction of the Franciscan Sisters of Baltimore. By 1908, the school had 135 students enrolled, and most of those children were the Remington ruffians who had been expelled from public school. The student body increased remarkably over the next six years, and the church decided it needed a dedicated building to handle the expansion in enrollment. SS Philip and James was finally out of debt by this time, and Father John Edward Wade, then pastor of the church, decided to purchase a piece of property on the corner of Maryland and Twenty-seventh for a school, which moved the facilities a little closer to the Remington community. Architect Hugh Ignatius Kavanagh, who was chosen to design the school, decided to have the name Peabody Heights Academy engraved over the entrance. Peabody Heights was the name of the neighborhood before it became a part of Charles Village. No one ever called the school by this name, however, but the building still exists with the engraving prominently displayed.

Supported by a parish of nearly two thousand, the school opened in September 1917 for grades K–8. A certain portion of the youngest

Eugene Sattler (front) with his first grade classmates at SS Philip and James. I wonder if his tie made it through recess? *Courtesy of Eugene Sattler.*

Opened in 1917 at the corner of Maryland and Twenty-seventh in the now defunct neighborhood of Peabody Heights, the Peabody Heights Academy served the Remington Catholic community youth from grades K–8. *Courtesy of SSPJ.*

The Gibbons Guild, an adjunct of SS Philip and James, operated in a building at Hampden and Twenty-ninth. It provided daycare for working parents. *Courtesy of Eugene Stattler.*

Remington children, however, were still without a facility. When both parents were forced to work during lean times, the children would be left with relatives or even on their own. So the women of SS Philip and James created the Gibbons Guild, a daycare/kindergarten facility that was housed on the corner of Hampden and Twenty-ninth Streets in Remington proper. By the early 1920s, the Guild had enrolled over fifty children and served over seventeen hundred meals to the local youngsters.

Other Remington churches supported community efforts and served moderate congregations. The Keen Memorial Baptist Church, which is no longer in existence, presented annual carnivals and picnics; the Oak Street AME provided sanctuary for the neighborhood's underserved black population; and the Bethany United Evangelical Church, which moved into the old Guardian Angel spot, served the north Remington population.

## COMMUNITY SCHOOL

Tom Culotta's loyalty to Remington has spanned several decades. Even when the neighborhood rejected his efforts to help those considered high-

Remington children never had a neighborhood public school and had to walk or ride to other neighborhoods to attend. This resulted in a high dropout rate for Remington teenagers. Tom Culotta started the Community Survival School to encourage community youth to complete their education. *Author's collection.*

risk residents, he forged ahead, and the Community School is the result of his perseverance.

The corner building on Lorraine and Howard now stands empty, but in the late 1970s, it was the home of the Community Survival Center. The community center was a popular haven for Remington's troubled youth, and Tom Culotta was its director. Tom was a welcome sight to parents concerned with juvenile crime and the high drop-out rate of their children. He began a series of programs that included overnight camping trips and visits to the Maryland Penitentiary to help steer the teens in a more positive direction. The center also provided adult residents with legal assistance and operated a food co-op. His warm welcome, however, was short-lived.

In the summer of 1978, twenty-year-old William Patrick "Patty" Meyers was shot by a police officer in front of the Beefmaster's Restaurant (now Meet 27) on the corner of Howard and Twenty-seventh. Tom witnessed the incident and immediately began picketing police headquarters over what he termed an "unjustifiable" homicide. His actions became a point of contention with some older residents, but it was the success of his food co-op that garnered the most resentment from one of his neighbors.

The co-op was in competition with a grocery store owned by the community center's landlord, and Tom suddenly found himself facing zoning violations because the building was zoned residential. Neighbors who formerly supported him wanted him out because of the teenagers loitering and fighting in front of the building. Councilwoman Mary Pat Clarke, also an original supporter of the initiative, questioned Tom's motives, stating she was not convinced that it was a community-based organization but rather "a one-man operation." Reverend Thomas Hudson, then rector of the Guardian Angel Episcopal Church who had never visited the center, simply hated its name. But Tom still had his supporters, and he was greatly admired by the center's youthful patrons.

The center then found accommodation on the 200 block of West Twenty-fifth Street where the co-op thrived and Tom's youth-based programs were gaining positive results. Tom was still vocally active in Remington's other concerns, and he became president of the Greater Homewood Community Corporation. Once again, he and city officials collided when the Department of Housing made plans to renovate the houses on the 2800 block of Remington Avenue without properly notifying the tenants.

In 1984, the Neighborhood Progress Administration (NPA), a super-agency under the Department of Housing and the Mayor's Office of Manpower Resources, had plans to rehabilitate the houses using local unskilled labor. The NPA stated it would provide "job training" for low-income residents of Remington to learn construction. They would be paid a $30.00-per-week stipend during a six-week training course and eventually earn $3.50 per hour. A training program never materialized. The NPA stated they were unable to locate any residents who would qualify for such a program and would look outside the neighborhood for trainees. Tom was outraged, stating he would provide eligible workers if the city would "create a bona fide training program," but the jobs never appeared. Today, the houses are again being rehabilitated under Baltimore City's "Vacants-to-Value" initiative and private developers, and they're looking pretty good.

Tom began focusing more on the educational opportunities he could provide and moved his school to its present location on Huntingdon Avenue, renaming it the Community School. The school, which combines academic and mentoring programs, offers full-time day classes to youth ages fifteen to eighteen. The curriculum is designed to prepare students to pass the GED exam and eventually enroll in college. It is governed by a community Board

Tom Culotta is community activist, children's advocate and devoted teacher and friend to generations of Remingtonians. He is pictured here receiving a congratulatory embrace from Councilwoman Mary Pat Clark. *Author's collection.*

of Trustees with the active support and involvement of a Board of Advisers, sponsors, students, parents, alumni and supporters from both Remington and beyond. Many Remington adults still owe a debt of gratitude to Tom and the school for enriching their lives.

## ATHLETICS AND SOCIAL CLUBS

Some Remingtonians found more productive ways of releasing youthful energy outside of hoodlumism. Athletic clubs were prolific throughout the community and nearby neighborhoods, leading to a more organized form of roughhousing that was encouraged by parents and the church leaders. The Remington A.C. hosted many ballgames on the Remington Oval, and the Justice family boys were always found on the field. Footballers had their own field, on which many a Mooney could be seen tossing the ball. Sometimes it was hard to get enough players from the neighborhood, so the boys would travel over one of the many bridges and join athletic clubs

Organized athletics, such as the Keswick Athletic Club, played a major part in the lives of young Remingtonians. When there was a shortage of players, some would wander "over the bridge" to join neighboring teams. *Courtesy of Ken Walters.*

Local businesses, such as the Mart Men's Shop, encouraged organized athletics by supporting the teams. Of course, it was also a useful form of advertisement. George Mooney (top row, second from right) was one of the many young Remingtonians who served in World War II. *Courtesy of Ken Walters.*

The Remington Athletic Club was always looking for a few good men to spar against in Wyman Park baseball. However, records indicate that losses outweighed wins during their tenure. Most of these boys would be enlisted in the Armed Forces in the coming years. *The Palmer Collection.*

formed in other neighborhoods, even though rivalry continued off the field. Teams with names like the Oaks Athletic Association, the Remington Juniors, Keswick A.C. and Wyman Park Baseball could be found practicing on the Sisson Street fields or in Wyman Park. The athletic clubs produced some decent pitchers, like Lefty Russell and Tom Phoebus, who both played for the Orioles in various eras, but the Remington clubs usually ended up with a losing streak during the season.

The waterways that ran throughout Remington provided relief from the miserable Baltimore summer heat as well as providing ice skating opportunities in winter. The streams and ponds were a lot safer than the quarries or the Jones Falls, but they also caused flooding and disease, as we shall see. One of the ponds most favored by the community was Sumwalt's ice pond located near Remington and Thirtieth Street. Originally named Edwards Run, the stream traversed south Remington to Glen Edwards Avenue and flowed into the Jones Falls. The run was on the property of David S. Sumwalt, a quarryman who, like many of his co-workers, sought a less dangerous occupation. Figuring blocks of ice were less threatening than blocks of granite, Sumwalt started an icehouse in the 1840s, one of the pioneers of a lucrative occupation that

employed a very large capital and many laborers, so he was pretty well liked in the community. It was his ice pond, however, that endeared him to many Remington boys, when it opened as a public pool in the late 1890s. Yes, fellow Remingtonians, we once had a swimming pool! In July 1899, the Playground Association opened the pool for boys only. The entry fee was one cent, but the penniless were allowed in anyway. Over two hundred boys used the pool from July to September of that year, and it was estimated over two thousand swims were taken. It cost the association sixty-five dollars in expenses, but it was the better alternative to the round falls, where the Remington and Hampden boys often engaged in fisticuffs.

At the turn of the twentieth century, Wyman Park Lanes provided league competition for duckpin bowling, a favored sport of Baltimoreans citywide. Many local bowling leagues were formed and played there.

*Top*: Remingtonians seem to have had a penchant for horses, whether for a short ride through Wyman Park… *The Palmer Collection.*

*Bottom*: Or waiting for the "pony man" to arrive for a day of fun. *Courtesy of Deborah Wiles.*

One activity that Remington neighbors always appreciated was horseback riding. There were many paths throughout the surrounding parkland, and stables in the area would rent their livestock to residents or visitors for a brisk ride through Wyman Park and undeveloped open areas. As the community became more populated, the stables disappeared, but local children were treated to pony rides by horse owners who visited the neighborhood. Cowboy costumes were distributed to the youngsters so they could have their photos taken. This practice continued to the 1980s, so there are many generations of cowboy and cowgirl images floating around Remington.

Social and political organizations, such as the Cresmont Social Club and the Huntingdon Democratic Club, were formed by the older residents who enjoyed the camaraderie of their neighbors in a communal setting. Eventually, community organizations, such as the Greater Remington Improvement Association and the Remington Neighborhood Alliance, developed and provided a forum for the neighborhood to interact not only with each other but also with the city as a whole.

CHAPTER 4

# THE SKEETER SCARE OF 1915

## U.S. Marine Hospital and Community Health

*My Dear General Gorgas: Bearing in mind the very admirable work which you
accomplished for the Government in the Canal zone, I am writing you in regard to
a matter of very deep interest to me as a Baltimorean. Confirming our telephone
conversation this morning, I beg to say that I am contemplating an anti-mosquito
crusade in Baltimore, but, so far as I am aware, we have no one here who is
familiar with the proper method of procedure and capable of carrying it out.*

*Yours Very Truly,*
*James H. Preston, Mayor*

As the Great War in Europe was escalating, Baltimore was abuzz.
Not with concern over U.S. involvement in the conflict, but with
mosquitoes. Mayor Preston had written to the surgeon-general of the
United States Army, William C. Gorgas, asking for help in exterminating
the mosquito population.

Gorgas had spearheaded a campaign against the yellow-fever carriers
in the Panama Canal, and Preston hoped he would be able to cure the
Baltimore blight. Gorgas directed Dr. Henry R. Carter, head of the U.S.
Marine Hospital located in Remington, to investigate the problem. Carter
had worked with Gorgas in the Panama Canal and in 1903 conducted
extensive research on the Baltimore mosquito. He assured the mayor
and the city that Baltimore mosquitoes were "harmless," except where
the Jones Falls flowed through the northernmost part of Remington.
However, Carter was convalescing at Johns Hopkins Hospital and could

not physically take part in the eradication program. Instead, William D. Wrightson, who also served with Gorgas in Panama, was appointed to oversee the physical operation.

Wrightson, a Baltimore native, was also son-in-law to Gorgas and would again serve under him in the U.S. Army Sanitary Corps when the United States entered the war. He was supervising a similar operation in New Orleans when he accepted the position. On his way to Baltimore, however, he was stricken with appendicitis and had to convalesce in a Washington, D.C. hospital. It seemed the mayor was unable to raise the army he need to fight the 'skeeter war. Finally, the commissioner of street cleaning, William A. Larkins, was appointed temporary supervisor in March 1915. One of his first stops was Remington.

Conditions were perfect for mosquito breeding as most of the northern portion of the community was in the first stages of development, and construction had left large pools of rainwater to accumulate on the planned lots. In addition, houses along the Twenty-eighth and Twenty-ninth Street corridor were five feet below street level due to roadwork, and the swimming pool that entertained the boys in the 1890s was overflowing into the yards of these homes. Feather beds, mattresses and tables were found to be floating about with outhouses. Water was so deep in some areas that children were playing on rooftops. Larkin, along with a couple city engineers, decided that draining and sewering the standing water was the best line of attack, and the mayor agreed. He had been trying to budget for sanitation improvement in Remington since he began his term, and this looked like an opportunity to kill two 'skeeters with one blow. The task proved formidable as new infestations along the Stony Run and Jones Falls were discovered. Remingtonians were worried about malaria from the Jones Falls mosquitoes, although they had been abiding the pests for generations. The Public Health Service announced that Sumwalt Pond, then owned by the City Dairy Company, was capable of developing enough mosquitoes to infest half of Baltimore. To allay some fears, Larkin had Sumwalt Pond drained and filled immediately. All through that spring and summer, city workers crowded the streets of Remington, pouring kerosene in small pools of water, draining the larger ponds and handing out thousands of leaflets telling the community how to combat the thick clouds of the critters that had descended on the neighborhood.

As fall approached, the mayor was getting frustrated by the campaign's lack of cooperation from Baltimore citizens and started fining householders that maintained mosquito-breeding places on their property under an ordinance he had passed that summer. Remingtonians were outraged that they were being targeted as the culprits in the matter and demanded the mayor hold to his promise of a new sewer line for Remington Avenue. Neither side budged in their demands as the war on mosquitoes continued until winter when most of the pests lay dormant.

As new development was being completed in north Remington, some of the mosquito population abated, but we better be careful as we approach the Stony Run, because those little bloodsuckers are still about!

## THE U.S. MARINE HOSPITAL

By 1922, the residents along Remington Avenue no longer had to contend with Sumwalt Pond, but their street was in bad shape. The city had not fulfilled its promise of a sewer, and conditions were awful. Residents on the east side of the 3000 block had been complaining for years about the unsanitary conditions due to lack of sewerage facilities. Instead, the houses were connected with a common drainpipe, with a cesspool in an alley in the rear of Thirty-first Street. The draining ran into a wooden trough, the sides of which were rotted, extending into Remington Avenue. There was standing water in it nearly all the time, and it was up to residents to clean it out, unless there was a hard rain to wash it out. Rubbish and dead rats could be found clogging the cesspool, and the odor was outrageous. Fearful of typhoid and other diseases, the neighborhood demanded its sewer, and the commissioner of health agreed. A new system was being installed that would service the area from Thirty-sixth Street in Hampden all the way to the city line, and Remington just had to wait its turn. In the meantime, all those houses that had been under water during the 'skeeter scare were being torn down to make way for commercial development, so streets would be regraded and paved to help with the runoff. Well, this is just icky, so let's walk a little farther north and see if we can find something a little more pleasant.

Aha! The site of the old U.S. Marine Hospital, now owned by the ubiquitous Johns Hopkins University system. Built in 1880s on part of William Remington's wooded estate, it was quickly occupied by soldiers in war and peace and constantly overcrowded. When these types of hospitals first started in 1798, they were exclusively for sailors of the merchant marines, who, before that time, depended upon public charity when they became ill. But the scope of marine hospitals kept expanding to include government employees injured at work, fishermen, the Coast Guard and their families and all members of the armed forces. So while the two brick buildings with their one-hundred-bed capacity served their purpose through the Spanish-American War with no problem, the little hospital was overwhelmed by the number of patients of admitted during World War I. Additional frame buildings were constructed, but the overcrowding was untenable and the building all but abandoned by 1920.

Plans for a new building started as early as 1922, and the hospital was reopened after the installation of new medical equipment. Governmental infighting and economic deficiency delayed the plans for further improvement, and the wooden structures became housing for the few doctors and nurses who remained to serve patients convalescing there. Expansion was hampered by the Johns Hopkins University's refusal to sell to the hospital a strip of land on the south side of the proposed structure, and construction was delayed for over a year while condemnation proceedings were fought out in federal court. Finally, at a cost of about $1 million, the old buildings were razed and a seven-story brick building was completed in 1934. By the time of World War II, the capacity was 380 beds, with room for 120 additional beds in other parts of the structure.

On the hospital grounds, consisting of about seven acres, there were green lawns, gardens and trees, in addition to the doctors' housing. There were about forty doctors working during wartime, but less than half could be accommodated by the buildings, and only half of the nursing staff had rooms at the facility. A total staff of 445 was required to operate the hospital. The U.S. marine hospitals worked under the auspices of the United States Public Health Service, and the physicians had rank, pay and living allowances corresponding to those of the armed services and wore insignia and uniforms of the navy.

The surgeons at the new hospital perfected surgical techniques on war injuries that would later be applied in civilian hospitals after the war, and the facility was unusually well equipped for treatment of cancer. There were also plastic surgeons who worked in conjunction with the dental clinic on many patients whose faces were ravaged by war or disease. The hospital also kept frozen a rare supply of yellow fever serum. Obviously, not for use by Remingtonians since we only had "harmless" mosquitoes!

*Opposite, top*: The old wooden structure of the original U.S. Marine Hospital was in dire need of repair, as seen in this 1931 photo. With the increased United States' involvement in World War II, it was decided that new structures would be necessary. *The Palmer Collection.*

*Opposite, bottom*: This photo of USMH staff was probably taken after the dedication of the new building. *The Palmer Collection.*

Some of the staff was composed of social workers who were frequently called on to act as intermediaries in the psychological dramas that war produced. There were also the Red Cross Gray Ladies, who started volunteering at the hospital before the war and continued their service throughout the conflict by writing letters, sending telegrams, running errands and distributing reading materials. Every once in a while, they would also show movies and make gifts for the patients confined there for the holidays.

There was no shortage of patients throughout the 1950s and 1960s, but things were beginning to fall apart at the seams by the 1970s when federal funding started dwindling during the recession. Much of the hospital's medical staff had left, and residency programs were reduced or eliminated. The bed count was reduced to a mere 161, and two of the seven floors were closed. The cancer research center was relocated to the University of Maryland.

It looked like the end of the hospital in the 1980s when President Reagan wanted it closed, but a compromise in Congress made it possible for the facility to convert to private use. In the last years of the 1970s, about thirty percent of its activities benefited the Remington community, providing a health clinic, mental health services, an alcoholism treatment center focusing on teenagers, a geriatric rehabilitation center and programs in psychiatry and occupational safety and health. Eventually, the building was sold to the Johns Hopkins University for administrative offices, and the clinics are serviced by Johns Hopkins community physicians. Some of the original public works artwork of the 1930s is still displayed on the lobby walls. Isn't it funny that after a huge legal battle to wrest a tiny strip of land from the school, the university ended up owning the entire facility?

# THE JOHNS HOPKINS COLORED ORPHAN ASYLUM

Let's go investigate that little strip of land the hospital had to sue over. In his original will establishing the Johns Hopkins Hospital, Mr. Johns Hopkins expressed the wish that provision be made for the care of "colored orphan children" and for "destitute colored children" in a building separate from the main hospital in east Baltimore. In April 1875, Johns Hopkins Hospital trustees took over the shelter for colored orphans located in the 200 block of West Biddle Street that was in financial trouble, and six months later, the building had been renovated. It was able to house twenty-six children and was operating within the allotted budget. The number of children increased to between fifty and sixty ten years later, but by 1888, the house had to reduce the number of occupants back to about twenty-five because of the inadequacy of the facilities. In 1894, the trustees decided to move the orphan asylum to a new site at Remington Avenue and King Street (now Thirty-first Street).

An existing building was purchased for $18,500, and another $30,500 was appropriated for construction of an addition. The asylum was under the general supervision of a committee of four hospital trustees and a Board of Lady Managers that functioned under the policy decisions of the trustee committee. The activities of the orphan asylum expanded for a few years, but evidently there were problems, for in 1904 the kindergarten was abolished, and later, efforts were made to have the education of the children, which had been the responsibility of the staff of the asylum, taken over by the public school system. It was not until 1909, however, that some of the orphans were sent to a nearby public school. Clearly, the orphan asylum was not a highly successful operation.

In 1913, Winford Smith, who was administratively responsible for this ancillary institution, presented a committee report to the Board of Trustees of the hospital. The committee believed that the facility could be better used as a school for convalescent crippled children operated by and in connection with the Johns Hopkins Hospital. It was proposed that the name be changed to the Convalescent Home for Crippled Colored Children, but since the activities of the institution continued to contain some elements of an orphanage, it was commonly designated simply "The Colored Home." They really were politically incorrect back then!

Over the years, the home had come to house only girls, and at the time of the conversion to the convalescent home, there were forty girls living there who were all placed as domestic servants in private homes. An annual report of the Johns Hopkins Hospital for 1914 stated that the care and training the girls received at the facility was not altogether satisfactory, and it seemed a wise move to have it converted into a convalescent hospital for handicapped children.

During the first full year of its operation as a convalescent home, eighty-one children received treatment for a total of 8,079 days at an average daily cost of $1.73. Children were given not only medical and nursing care but some school instruction as well. With the United States' involvement in World War I, the departure of the base hospital unit for France and its attendant shortage of physicians and nurses at Hopkins, as well as the growing annual deficit of the Hospital, the Board of Trustees reluctantly decided to close the school and convalescent home for crippled children temporarily. Doubtless the proximity of the Children's Hospital School, a facility for the treatment of crippled children located on Greenspring Avenue on the west side of the Jones Falls, entered into the decision to close this small and ineffective medical unit. A number of proposals were received from the federal government concerning possible uses of the premises for war casualties, but it was hoped that the home would soon be reopened by the Johns Hopkins Hospital to serve its original purpose. Unfortunately, this was never accomplished because the U.S. Marine Hospital wanted the property and successfully sued to have the property condemned for its use. The Johns Hopkins Hospital continued to regard the orphans who had been placed in private homes as wards and exercised a degree of surveillance over them through a social worker on the Johns Hopkins Hospital staff.

During the transition between the closing of the convalescent home and the condemnation of the property, Johns Hopkins University used one of the buildings on the property as a "psychological research laboratory," according to one of the local newspapers, but no archivist at the university has been able to confirm this. Spooky!

CHAPTER 5

# THE THREE LIVES OF REMINGTON

## *Developing Diversity*

*John Schultheis stared at Baltimore County Court Clerk John W. Shanklin with contempt. How dare this miserable civil servant deny his application for a license? Hadn't he proven his beloved restaurant fell outside the prohibited area? If Shanklin wanted a fight, then he would get one. Schultheis went to see the judge.*

So, have we learned anything at this point in our magical history tour? I hope so, because all this walking through centuries is exhausting! One thing that should be apparent by now is the diversity of the neighborhood. We visited south Remington and Good Husbands' Row, with its mixture of Irish and Italian families; the north with its Wyman Park, Stony Run and undeveloped Bay Estate; and the central area, with its crazy infrastructure of bridges and railroads. But as I stated before, Remington is people, so let's meet some of them!

## LITTLE LITTLE ITALY

Back over Sisson Street Bridge to south Remington, where the aroma of marinara wafts down from Corky's Restaurant. It wasn't too long ago that the entire neighborhood smelled like an Italian restaurant as the immigrants who worked the quarries and railroads settled here. Even the architecture was Italianate, with two-story homes appearing around Turner Place (named for developer Joseph Turner), which today is the block formed by the two sides of Fawcett Street. We can see where Emmor Fawcett bought his property right in front of the Maryland Construction Company. Emmor was a self-confirmed capitalist, as he stated on the 1880 census. He made a lot of money suing railroads and other capitalists, including his neighbor, Nathan Haines. Haines owned a few rental properties on Glen Edwards Avenue and once bought shares of a bogus silver mine in Arizona from Fawcett. I don't think they were very friendly neighbors.

The American Ice Company is located on a Nathan Haines property, right across the street from Turner Place. Nathan's widow, Elizabeth, sold the property to the American Ice Company of New Jersey in 1904 for $14,000. The American Ice Company had its own little train that ran to the warehouse and connected to the B&O line to ship the ice. The icehouse is still in existence but has become the shop of Thomas Brown, Woodwright LLC, who has made Baltimore's best historically accurate doors and shutters (among a thousand other things, as long as it's wood) for over twenty years.

We could walk to the west side of Twenty-third Street to see if we can spot any rocks leftover from Hugh Sisson's stone yard, but, alas, the B&O claimed it long ago. We can, however, visit the location of Sisson's rental properties in Jefferson Place.

You would be unable to tell from the commercialization of Howard Street that this area had once supported over one hundred town houses. Gone are the large livery stable and blacksmith shop and two-story Italianate dwellings owned by Mr. Mitchell in 1884, almost all of the Sisson rental properties and the oyster-house that John Schultheis fought so hard to get licensed in 1888. But there are a few remnants of the development that existed in the early 1900s located on 2200 block of Huntingdon Avenue behind Corky's (which used to be more aptly named DeLuca's).

Jefferson Place and Oak Street (now Howard Street) were always a bit commercial with its numerous taverns and eateries. One of the main reasons for Remington's taverns being located on the south side was an act passed in 1882 that prohibited the issuing of licenses for the sale of "spirituous and fermented liquors" within three-quarters mile of the Mount Vernon Mills. John Schultheis was so determined to open his restaurant that he hired the county surveyor to measure the distance from his place to the nearest point of the Mount Vernon factory buildings. The surveyor found that the restaurant would lie ten inches outside the prohibited area, so Schultheis reapplied for the license and was again turned down by the county clerk. The clerk maintained that a true reading of the statute meant the distance

Elizabeth Haines, widow of real estate developer Nathan Haines, sold this entire block of property to the American Ice Company in 1904. The icehouse was a favored spot for the locals to walk through during hot and humid summers. Ice would be delivered by horse cart to families requesting the service, but those who were economically handicapped would often find means of relieving the cart of some of its contents en route. *Author's collection.*

from the Mount Vernon Mills factory grounds, not the buildings. Schultheis had enough of this nonsense and went before the court to compel the clerk to issue the license, and the court decided in favor of the restaurateur. I hope Mr. Schultheis was able to make a profit after paying all those court costs!

I guess we couldn't avoid noticing a replica of the Statue of Liberty on top of the Liberty Roofing Company building on Twenty-first Street, could we? The ten-foot-tall Miss Liberty glows at night and is a bit of a landmark in this portion of Remington. Nicholas Detorie Jr., the president of the business, really loved his liberty. If we go inside the building, we would see Nick's collection of Liberty coins and other Liberty memorabilia, including a clear plastic toilet seat inset with Liberty coins, that were gifts or his own investment. He even has a replica of the Liberty Bell that he loans out for parades. The business was started in 1932 by his father, an Italian immigrant who helped other immigrants find employment. His mother, Teresa DeLuca, owned the restaurant now called Corky's.

I think we should revisit Glen Edwards Avenue again and say hello to Michangelo Elmo. As we walk past the homes here, we can see why it was once called the "Italian colony" in the early 1900s. Names like Vicchio, Possidente, Bianzo, Austelio and Tambia were listed on the 1910 census. The Detories also lived here. Michelangelo Elmo and his wife, Rosa, emigrated from Italy in 1907 and were naturalized in 1928. They originally lived at 404 Glen Edwards Avenue, but the 1940 census shows they owned their house at 416 Fawcett Street, where they lived with two of their seven children, one of whom was seventeen-year-old Angelina. Michelangelo worked for the city as a street cleaner, Rosa was a picker at a cotton mill and Angelina worked in a laundry as a presser. Sometime between April 1940 and April 1942, Angela met and married Mason Phoebus. The couple were the parents of Orioles pitcher Tom Phoebus, a Remington celebrity famous for his no-hitter against Boston in 1968. See how those Remington athletic clubs paid off?

## GREATER REMINGTON

Back over the bridge we go to stroll along Sisson Street, another overly commercialized area that once contained residences, ball fields, the Sun Cab and High's Dairy. Remington had quite a few cow pastures owned by various commercial dairies, probably because we had so many ponds and undeveloped land they could access. The City Dairy Company, which assumed both the name and business of the Western Maryland Dairy Company, had a plant around Twenty-ninth Street and Remington Avenue on the old Sumwalt estate. Then there was Schier's Hygeia Dairy and store (the locals just called it "Hy's") on Sisson and Twenty-seventh Streets that was well known for its claim that it was the first to use sanitary and hygienic bottling for its products (get it, "Hygeia"—"hygienic"?). The company was owned by Oscar B. and Carl F. Schier, two brothers who emigrated from Germany in the early 1890s. They started out as confectioners before moving into the dairy business, where they pioneered the sale of pasteurized and bottled milk in the city and won a reputation for the quality of their ice cream products. The company maintained its own stables on Sisson Street to deliver the milk and employed wagon drivers who lived nearby. The most distinguishing feature of this building was the wooden horse's head that peeked out through the bricks. Carl Schier later became a director for the Western Maryland Dairy when that company assumed his business in 1922.

Sanitary Laundry and Dry Cleaning took over the building in the 1930s and provided employment for many Remingtonians, especially of the female persuasion. One of the specialized job opportunities the company offered, according to its advertisements, was the position of "bosom ironers." I bet that doesn't appear on many résumés today!

The site where the laundry stood is vacant now; the building was razed and the poor horse's head split in two and hauled off to the dump. Today, urban gardeners are starting to use the location under the guidance of Twenty-seventh Streeter Bill Cunningham. With so many avid gardeners participating, I'm predicting a bumper crop!

Across the street was once the location of High's Dairy store and plant, a local favorite, not only for its products but also for the number of job opportunities it offered. While we're on Twenty-seventh Street, let's amble eastward and see who else we might have seen in this era.

First we would spot Frank and Yetta Kane's Deli on our right. All but one of the neighborhood delis were owned by Jewish families who lived above their stores. A couple doors up is Piney's Tavern, next-door to Ken Walters's house. Mr. Walters used to make beer during Prohibition, and he would sell it to his friends, including Nick Dieter, who owned the tavern. Walters had knocked a hole in the wall behind the medicine chest in his bathroom so he could pass the beer through to Nick. On our left is Pipke's basement grocery store where Ken Walters Jr. went to work when he was fifteen years old. Oh, look across the street, it's Valenza's candy store! Practically every corner in this section has a store, and Valenza's, on Bernard (Miles) and Twenty-seventh, was the best loved by the neighborhood kids with its Tastykakes, pickled onions, Utz potato chips, penny candy and the glorious steel snowball machine. The Valenzas had been Remington "Bernarders," (dedicated residents of Bernard Avenue) since 1905, when Andrea Valenza emigrated from Italy to work on the Jones Falls railroads. He accrued enough money to open a shoe repair shop and trained son Joe and grandson Andrew to become cobblers. Joe eventually took over the shop, but Andrew hated the business. When Joe's wife, Angela, added penny candy and Utz chips to a display case in front of the shop, the shoe business took a back seat.

After Joe and Angela retired, Andrew and his wife, Patricia, moved in and made it a traditional corner store that served the immediate area, although their famous snowballs drew crowds from all points in the community. It was a sad day for Remington when they closed their store.

Al's Tavern (once owned by the Mooney clan, now operating as Three Mile House) is on the next block, but we might as well turn up

Now vacant, the Valenzas operated this corner store for generations, first as a shoe repair business and later as a popular variety store. *Author's collection.*

Huntingdon Avenue so we can stop and say hello to everyone at Sam & Angie's grocery store on the way past. It was *the* place to buy your meat in this area. But when Sam & Angie's became International Grocery in the early part of this century, Remington was going through one of its bad periods. One summer, temperatures rose so high in the store that the candy melted. The owner discovered the store's entire air conditioning system had been stolen.

Crossing over at Twenty-eighth Street, we pass the aptly named Hard Times Tavern, and farther north, on the corner of Twenty-ninth and Huntingdon, there is the A&P grocery store, with its landmark steeple, next to Goldberg's Hardware Store.

Most of these businesses no longer exist today. As Remington's Asian and Middle Eastern population skyrocketed, the few remaining corner stores became their business venues. Zoning laws and economic hardship prevented the reopening of some ventures that were the heart and soul of the Remington community. Let's have a moment of silence.

A Remington fixture since 1949, Sterling's on Twenty-ninth Street still serves the impossible-to-find fried hard crab. Yum! *Author's collection.*

Small businesses intersected with light industrial throughout Remington. The Walperts started their electrical contracting business in Baltimore in the 1920s and continue to operate from their Hampden Avenue location today. *Courtesy of Ronald Walpert.*

Well, they don't call it Greater Remington for nothing, so let us carry on.

Looking west toward the Twenty-ninth Street Bridge, you can see a couple businesses that have weathered the hard times. Long John's Pub has been in business seemingly forever. Phil Crouch bought the operation in the mid-1970s, and he still rules it with an iron fist. Sterling's Seafood, in business since 1949, still sells its famous seafood sub and crabs. Other, newer businesses line the south side of Twenty-ninth all the way to Sisson Street. Potts & Callahan, which assumed Peddicord's heavy equipment operations, governs the north side of the street. A quick peek down Hampden Avenue reveals Allan N. Walpert & Sons electrical contractors. The Walperts emigrated from Russia in 1903 to settle in Baltimore, where Allan Walpert plied his trade as an electrician. He opened his first shop in the 1920s, and the family has kept it in operation ever since.

Across the street from Walpert's is the old Ackerman residence, where Jim Gilpin was raised by his grandparents George (a brakeman for the railroad) and Katherine Ackerman. Jim's aunt Hazel also lived with them, and even through the Great Depression, everybody worked. Hazel was only sixteen in the 1930s when she found a job in a photography studio in downtown Baltimore. Like a lot of Remington men, Jim joined the armed forces, married his wife, Jane, and moved away from Remington after his discharge. He still has fond memories of growing up here, though.

Looking at Remington Groceries at the corner of Twenty-ninth and Huntingdon, we are reminded of the old T&T Food Market, once the domain of the "Devil of Remington," George Schedel. George was a crusty, Camel-smoking, rough-spoken curmudgeon with a heart of gold. As much as he screamed at his customers to quit talking and buy something, he would often let them pay "on the cuff," meaning he got paid when they got paid. Sometimes he never got paid. Natives fondly remember his store with the cracked, coffee-stained, glass-topped counter holding the metal rack piled high with glazed donuts. His broken register had its cash drawer permanently opened, and the meat case held its usual supply of bologna and cheese wheels. On Saturday mornings, the T&T was a circus, and George was its ringleader. It was more than a neighborhood food mart as it served as a meeting hall, stand-up restaurant, social club and entertainment center for over twenty-five years. While he probably made more money than the other corner stores, he also got robbed more often. The Twenty-ninth Street traffic brought some bad characters through the neighborhood, and thieves kept coming back to the T&T to empty George's register. He was once robbed seven times over a four-day period! He sold the store to his granddaughter and her husband in 1982 and died shortly thereafter, but the "Devil of Remington" is still with us in spirit.

If we were standing in the doorway of the T&T and looking east on Twenty-ninth past the Jaffes' liquor store, we would spot other spirits of Remington past: the Open House Coffee Shop, now the Papermoon; the Kayo gas station, now Pizza Boli's; and Jarman Pontiac, now Anderson Body Shop. Today, looking north on Huntingdon, we may spot Beth Barbush's front porch full of children practicing Porch Art, a program she runs with help from her Huntingdon Avenue friends and the Greater Remington Improvement Association. The program was developed to give the neighborhood children a consistent activity that demonstrated that people in the neighborhood care about them. The Maryland Institute College of Art also collaborates with the project, and Porch Art grew from eight kids to about thirty people each week.

One of the contributions these young artists make to the Huntingdon Avenue area is decorations for Hauntingdon, a Remington-unique Halloween festival initiated by Ms. Barbush that is as much anticipated as participated. The Porch Artists create scarecrows, masks and other decorations for this annual block party. This is a precursor to the extreme nightmare-before-Christmas decorating of Thirty-fourth Street in Hampden. I really don't know which is scarier.

Walking south from Twenty-ninth and Remington Avenue, we can see the eighty-five-year-old Baltimore Glass Company, which sits across the street from the row house in the 300 block of Twenty-seventh Street that was once owned by MacGregor Burns, a musician and Johns Hopkins graduate. Bands from around the country played in the basement of Burns's row house while passing through Baltimore. On the same block lives Jeffrey Blake, who still sits on his porch with his black Labrador keeping an eye out for trouble. He is a third-generation Remingtonian who plans on living here the rest of his life. A lot of us feel that way!

I'm starving, so let's stop in at the Papermoon Diner and see what's cooking.

No one traveling on Twenty-ninth Street can miss this place with its the yellow neon sign and ceramic cow. The interior is a riot of color with its purple ceiling, green walls, fans speckled with red and yellow polka dots and an eclectic collection of, well, I guess you would call it "stuff." Un Kim, a former deli owner, and Dan Robinson, a Maryland Institute graduate, bought the old Open House coffee shop, renovated it in less than a month and opened it in record time. Mr. Robinson designed the interior, and it has

*Above*: Some of the "stuff" that decorates the Papermoon Diner on Twenty-ninth Street. *Author's collection.*

*Opposite, top*: Many of the residents along the 2900 block of Huntingdon Avenue contribute to Hauntingdon by transforming their front porches into scary scenes. *Author's collection.*

*Opposite, bottom*: Porchless residences along Twenty-fourth Street in Little Little Italy find ways to contribute to the Remington love of Halloween. *Author's collection.*

become another Remington landmark. Un Kim would become a center of controversy for her unique developing efforts, as we shall see later on, but right now I'm ordering the Naked Cow!

Let's leave Greater Remington to see how things are developing up north.

# NORTH REMINGTON

Finally! The Jane Bay estate has settled and development is underway, but the Jane Bay Home for Boys is not one of the projects. Her will specifically

*Above*: Weather did not deter these fashionable young ladies from their stroll through the newly created Wyman Park. William Remington donated eleven acres of his property to its development. *Courtesy of SSPJ.*

*Left*: Married in 1916, the Palmers were one of the first couples to occupy the new houses on the 3100 block of Remington Avenue. *The Palmer Collection.*

stated that the trust was supposed to buy a piece of land in Baltimore County and erect the home, but we're not in Baltimore County anymore, Toto! We've been Baltimore City since 1888, so wherever the home goes, it's not going to be here. The trustees scrambled to look for a suitable venue for the building, and after thirty-seven years, the Jane Bay Hall (no longer a home for orphans) was going to be built at the McDonogh School for Boys for use as a dormitory. The building still stands on the campus and, appropriately, houses the archives and infirmary. Now what to do with the rest of her property…

As previously noted, some of Jane's land was condemned for use by the railroad and some was purchased by James Atkinson for his home near his quarry. The extension of Cedar Avenue (Wyman Park Drive) gobbled a small percentage of her property (and redefined Remington boundaries), and after the city turned down the trustees' purchase price, a huge amount of her land was condemned to add to Wyman Park. So the next time we travel down the Stony Run Trail, remember we're in Bay country!

In 1914, Charles E. Litzinger, a developer who made a fortune building houses in Hampden, dared to step over the bridge to buy thirty tracts of land for houses. These were to be the upscale, two-story "daylight houses" for which he was known. Daylight houses were those that had skylights on the top floor, and they sold fast. One of the first buyers of these houses were the Palmers.

Henry Harrison Palmer from Parkton was an engineer for the railroad when he met Florence E. Sunderland from Greater Remington. We don't know if it was a whirlwind courtship, but they married just when the Litzinger houses were on the market. The couple bought 3156 Remington (they would have been my next-door neighbors) and set up housekeeping. Florence was in heaven because she managed to "move up the hill" from her family's rented house on Bernard Street, a dream some Remingtonians held close to their hearts (some moved so far up the hill that they now live in Pennsylvania). Here she had the opportunity to take daily strolls or horseback rides through the park, associate with the Johns Hopkins University faculty and staff and watch performances given by those poor children at the Colored Orphan Asylum. She was now "affluent." OK, at this point we can stop the tape for a minute. Remember that just down the street there was an open sewer and pestilence, the U.S. Marine Hospital was overflowing with World War I patients, trains and trolleys were rolling down Remington and over the Huntingdon Viaduct and gangs were fighting on the nearby bridges. For a Bernarder, that was nothing; once a Bernarder, always a Bernarder was

Once a Bernarder, always a Bernarder was the motto of the residents on Bernard Street. Renamed Miles Avenue sometime after World War II, older Remingtonians still refer to it by its original name. *Courtesy Deborah Wiles.*

that street's motto. It was still home, and it was still Remington, so Florence embraced her new lifestyle, had a baby and moved her mother into the third bedroom. Who would want to live anywhere else?

The Palmers' only child, Dorothy, was much doted on. She wore the best clothes at Easter, took piano lessons, attended Sunday School around the corner at Keen Memorial Baptist Church, finished high school and was educated at the Girls Vocational Evening School, where

Perched on the backporch stairs in 1922, Dorothy Palmer displays her Easter Sunday best. The Palmers were considered "affluent" Remingtonians who occupied the "light houses" built by Charles Lightzinger in 1916. *The Palmer Collection.*

she studied secretarial skills and saw every performance of *La Scala* at the Lyric Opera House. She was a Remington debutante. She would live at 3156 Remington until her marriage in the late 1950s to Troy Thornberry, a widower several years her junior. The couple then lived at 3144 Remington Avenue, just a couple doors down from her family home. Dorothy lived in Remington until 2000, when she had to move because of ill health. She died in 2003.

Streetcars and bridges provided easy access for Remingtonians, like Dorothy Palmer and a friend, to explore the shopping opportunites in downtown Baltimore. *The Palmer Collection.*

Around the corner at 302 West Thirty-first lived the Sattlers, whose house was built by another developer during the same time period as the Palmers. Joseph Bernard Sattler was a telegraph operator who came from the Union Square area of Baltimore. The son of German immigrants, Joseph married Birdie Mae Manion in April 1919. Birdie Mae lived on the 2900 block of

Exhibiting the collegiate influence of the Johns Hopkins University, a student strikes a pose. *The Palmer Collection.*

Cedar Avenue, just a stone's throw from her future home. The couple had three children, Joseph, Elizabeth and Eugene, who all attended SS Philip and James Academy and, like many North Remingtonians, attended college. The boys joined the armed services, and Betty became a nurse at the nearby Union Memorial Hospital.

There has always been a bit of snobbery among north Remingtonians because they lived "on the hill," probably a throwback to the days when quarrymen lived down in the valley and quarry owners lived farther uphill. Also, unlike the neighborhood south of Thirtieth Street, the area had and still has no major commercial development.

The one aspect of daily living that prevailed throughout all sections of the Remington was laundry day. It was almost a pact among the women to do laundry on Monday while the children were in school and the husband was (hopefully) at work so they could get the clothes hung out to dry and have a chance to socialize over the backyard fences. Backyards were

*Top*: Mrs. Holden hangs laundry in her backyard. The Sattlers house is seen in the background. Gene Sattler recalls the laundry day process: "The cellar had two washtubs and a washing machine with a clothes wringer for wringing out the excess water. The clothes were taken outside to dry on the clothesline." *Courtesy of Fay Holden.*

*Bottom*: Overseeing the photography process, a grandmother watches from the summer kitchen. Screened-in back porches were a must to combat the inevitable Baltimore summer heat and humidity. *Courtesy of Deborah Wiles.*

*Opposite*: The Easter Parade was an occasion to display fashion finery. *The Palmer Collection.*

designated for gardens and clotheslines. In keeping with a long Baltimore tradition, most neighbors use their front porch to entertain and people watch. Even today, many Remingtonians eschew dryers, and rows of clothes can be seen drying in the wafting breeze as friends and neighbors sit in front of their homes to socialize.

While the North Remington women could be found gossiping around the clotheslines, the men could be found at Mitchell's saloon, which, according to a search of liquor licenses, opened at the end of 1934. Mitchell's was in business for almost forty years. Today that same corner bar/restaurant is now called the Dizz, managed by Remington's very own Elaine Stevens. Elaine is the granddaughter of George Schedel, so you know there's a little devil in her also! The Dizz regularly receives rave reviews, and people from all over the city enjoy wonderful food combined with wonderful prices. You should definitely make a point to stop in to say hello to Elaine and grab a burger.

The Palmers, Sattlers and their neighbors looked forward to any occasion to display their Sunday finery, and the best opportunity was

during the Easter Parade. The event became part of Baltimore's spring rite around the beginning of the 1900s, with activity initially centered around Mount Vernon Place. Following World War I, the crowds moved a few miles north on Charles Street to Wyman Park. The tradition became so ingrained after only a few years that many Easter Parade strollers turned out regularly, rain or shine. It was a fashion show and social gathering rolled into one. It was an after-church event where parishioners would parade from downtown Charles Street to Mount Royal Avenue to meet the processions from the uptown churches. Then

The Easter Parade on Charles Street was a high point of the Lenten season. Many Remingtonians were members of the SS Philip and James Catholic Church, seen undergoing development. *Courtesy of SSPJ.*

the procession would turn around and parade down to Mount Vernon Place. The crowds along Wyman Park and Charles Street were particularly dense, and Harrison Palmer probably perched little Dorothy, in all her finery, atop his shoulders so she could view the spectacle. The elite were always out in force, but the event drew the blue-collar crowd en masse, too. It was a social gathering for Remingtonians who had moved away from the neighborhood to get together with old friends they hadn't seen for awhile. In the 1950s, people began moving out of the city, television was the major attraction and the Easter Parade came to an end.

While we're standing in Wyman Park, let's walk around and see if we can find the man himself, William Remington.

## THE REMINGTONS

William Remington was living in Philadelphia, Pennsylvania, where he married Caroline Barney Williams from Baltimore. Only distantly related to the Remington gun manufacturing clan, William was not privy to the wealth of that branch of the family. It was Caroline who had the property and money, so when she wanted to return to Baltimore, William had little choice but to follow. The Remington estate, bought sometime around 1850, covered the approximate area between Thirty-first Street to Twenty-eighth Street and Huntingdon Avenue to Charles Street. Given the unspecified title of "merchant," it isn't certain what William actually did for a living. It may have been importing textiles, but more likely the family earned income from leasing their land. He did, at one time, petition to have his estate become the seat of Baltimore County but lost out to Towsontown. He also gave eleven acres of land to the city for the development of Homewood Park, now Wyman Park Dell, and paid for the laying out of Remington Avenue.

William and Caroline had three children, William Williams, Horace and Caroline R. It is known that Horace was a clerk in the St. James Hotel, William Williams worked for a bicycling manufacturer and we don't know what Caroline R. was up to. So where are these people

This is a portion of an 1876 map on which the Remington estate appears. It depicts the property of William Remington and his self-named street. *Author's collection.*

The members of this audience attending the dedication ceremony of the Lee and Jackson statue in 1948 included descendants of the two Confederate generals. Despite its controversial subject matter, the statue still stands on Wyman Park Drive. *Courtesy of John McGrain.*

living? We're standing at the foot of the notorious Jackson and Lee monument in Wyman Park Dell across from the upscale town homes on Wyman Parkway that were built in the early 1920s, and no Remingtons in sight. Time to check the phone directory. Aha! There he is—Wm. Remington, Charles Street. Wow, William Remington—for whom our little neighborhood is named—lived in Charles Village! What irony.

The Remington boys, William and Horace, died young and childless, so the family line ended in the 1890s with the death of William Remington Sr. With the end of our namesake so ends our magical history tour. Don't forget to visit the Baltimore Streetcar Museum for your trolley ride!

CHAPTER 6

# FLEETING PROSPERITY

## A Mirror to the City

*The teenager buying the pack of Marlboros looked at the reporter in amazement. What was he talking about? What crime? So what if he never graduated high school, he had a job stocking shelves at High's Dairy and earned enough for his cigarettes and beer. All this talk about the neighborhood going downhill was just nonsense. He was born and raised here; he'd never leave.*

One of the largest components in the changing demographics of Remington was World War II. Many young men from the neighborhood eagerly enlisted, and a large number of them never returned from overseas. Those that did return either clung to their roots and settled back into civilian life by raising their families in Remington or, disillusioned by the war, pulled up stakes to live in suburbia on the GI Bill.

A memorial dedicated to those who served in the conflagration can be found at the corner of Wyman Park and San Martin on the Homewood Campus of Johns Hopkins University. One side of the memorial reads: "To the Men and Women of the Community Whose Duty and Devotion with Their Services in World War II Were Not Given in Vain," and the other side is a bronze plaque listing the names of those who served. Many of those names are familiar to Remingtonians: George and John Mooney; Ford G. and Harry Wilgis; Nicholas and Pasqual Possidente; John, Nick and Richard Detorie; and my cousins, William, Wilbert and Calvert Ambrose.

From the 1950s through the 1970s, Baltimoreans were worried. Protests over the Vietnam War, racial bigotry and economic inequality produced

*Left:* These four friends gathered for an after-game photo. Together, they joined the armed forces in World War II, but not all of them returned from conflict. *Courtesy of Ken Walters.*

*Below:* The neighborhood men who served in World War II are memorialized on this edifice. *Author's collection.*

a deeply disturbing violence. Desegregation of schools, department stores and public facilities did not always bring social harmony. Most communities remained all black or all white, and Jews were excluded from some neighborhoods and organizations. Many white people, of all income groups, believed that Baltimore was doomed, and they fled to the suburbs. Industries were also abandoning the city.

The 1960s and '70s were a period of rapid change for Remington. For over a century, Remingtonians had relied on steady jobs at the quarries, mills and factories, but those jobs were fading fast. Strapped for cash, residents were unable to afford home improvements, and the quality of housing declined. With little educational attainment, residents couldn't find new jobs. The economic downturn increased neighborhood crime, substance abuse, alcoholism and a dependence on social welfare programs. But the drug problem was the most alarming. Sharon Skarbelis, president of the Remington Improvement Association, was a resident on Cresmont Avenue in North Remington, when she noticed that teenagers from Greater Remington were disappearing into the Stony Run hollow to inhale tourlo, a chemical cleaning solvent. Inhalant abuse was a precursor to the harder drugs that would invade Remington. The tourlo was cheap and easy to find as it was used in automobile repair shops, and if it was one thing Remington was never lacking, it was auto repair shops. The chemical was also used in various industrial plants in the Jones Falls Valley, and boys would climb fences and steal the liquid from the drums that had to be stored outside because it was so flammable. Committees were formed to discuss the problem and decided that it was the result of uncaring parents who were unemployed and had their own alcohol abuse to overcome. The Keen Memorial Baptist Church hosted the House Center, Inc., the focus of which was on preventing access to the inhalants.

This social upheaval caused many people to leave Remington to seek opportunities elsewhere. Between 1960 and 1970, the neighborhood's population declined by 14 percent to total 3,842, according to the 1970 census. A 1980 study by Greater Homewood Community Corporation detailed Remington's lack of a drugstore, supermarket, fire station and school and noted that 80 percent of the population never finished high school. The report also mentioned an increase in vacant housing and a marked lack of recreational space.

During this time, several attempts were made to combat the decline of the neighborhood. The Remington Improvement Association was created to address quality of life issues. The neighborhood successfully lobbied the city to build a new community center, and the Wyman Park Multipurpose Center opened in August 1977 on West Thirtieth Street.

The multi-purpose center, tucked away behind Potts & Callahan on the edge of Wyman Park south, offered a variety of new services for neighborhood residents and served as the new base of operations for a number of programs that had existed in the area for some time. The Greater Homewood Mayor's Station operated from the center under the administration of Donna Keck. The center also had a recreation program that revolved around a gymnasium. The gym was open weekdays from 3:00 p.m. until 10:00 p.m., with afternoon hours reserved for children age twelve and under, leaving the evening hours open for teenagers and adults. Upon the gym's opening, over four hundred young people immediately signed up for the program, proving how starved the area's youth were for a place of recreation. The Action in Maturity offices, along with the senior citizens' Eating Together program, were also located in the center. In addition, every Tuesday and Thursday, a representative from the Food Stamp Outreach program was there to provide information about and to accept applications for food stamps. A tutorial program that had operated out of Keen Memorial Baptist Church (now Greater Faith Baptist) moved its operations there, and the center council developed a daycare program that provided three beautifully designed rooms opening into play areas for the tending of two- to four-year-olds. Part of the center's lobby became a library, and meeting rooms were available for community groups and special events. All things looked bright and sunny as the community tried to rally against the rising tide of economic and social woes, but it was apparent that something wasn't quite right with the building.

Remember way back in the early part of our tour when I mentioned how the city used Atkinson's quarry to dump the debris of the Great Fire of 1904? Well, guess where the center was sitting? That's correct, right on top of it. Ever since its opening, the center had been sinking because pockets of air in the landfill were collapsing, and the northern quarter of the center was settling at an alarming rate. Cracks were appearing in the floor and walls. The city sent in inspectors who declared the building safe, but something would have to be done to shore up the building. The city had already spent hundreds of thousands of dollars in grouting and maintenance, and the occupants of the center believed they would have to leave, just when the programs were proving beneficial to Remington. Luckily, Mayor Schaefer was in office, and developers were his friends. He got Whiting-Turner, a huge Baltimore contractor, to do the work for free, but the center's residents would have to be relocated. In the interim, some

OCTOBER 1977

# neighbors

PUBLISHED QUARTERLY BY THE GREATER HOMEWOOD COMMUNITY CORPORATION

REMINGTON'S HISTORY ● HOW I SPENT MY SUMMER VACATION ● EASTERN HIGH SCHOOL TASK FORCE ● GETTING TO SCHOOL ● THE TALE OF THE RATS AND THE TRACKS ● MULTI-PURPOSE CENTER ● & AROUND THE NEIGHBORHOOD

Even with today's prolific Internet access, most older residents prefer receiving community news in hard copy. This issue of *Neighbors*, one of the former community publications, celebrated the history of the community and shows Father Kromer leading the neighborhood children to school. *Courtesy of Betsy Childs.*

of the programs were discontinued and never returned to the site. Some of the building would eventually become the home of the GreenMount School, a private charter enterprise.

In addition to social programs, Linda Cox and others created a community newsletter, called the *Remington Rambler*, and began distributing it to their neighbors, which was read as avidly as the *Wall Street Journal*. The Greater Homewood Community Corporation also printed a newsletter called *Neighbors*, which included Remington stories and news.

Despite the community commitment, businesses were closing all over Remington. The two Cadillac art deco–style showrooms at the corner of Twenty-ninth and Remington were abandoned, corner stores were left vacant as family owners moved out of the city and homes were falling into decline. The only population increase in Remington was rats.

In 1983, Baltimore City had identified over 120 areas in Remington that were severely infested with rats. The neighborhood started an all-out warfare against the rat population using any means necessary. They used poison, brooms, rakes and shovels against the bold vermin that would brazenly stroll down the streets and alleys. The neighborhood initiative, with a little help from Baltimore's "Rat Rubout" program, distributed packets of poison and metal trash cans and provided dumpsters for the collection of trash. By 1987, the community cautiously declared the eradication a success and held a "rat bash" party at Keen Memorial Baptist Church. The party included a large rat piñata, made out of shopping bags and papier-mâché by Remington artist Kai Brouard, who called his creation "Ratso." Luckily, the real rats were easier to kill than Ratso. Children from the Remington Clean Kids squad took turns bashing Ratso with a stick, with no success. Kai Brouard himself gave it his best but also failed. Finally, the kids were allowed to rip it open with their hands, which proved to be the only way to get to the candy inside.

The expansion of the Johns Hopkins University Homewood campus was another sticking point for Remingtonians. There was always a love/hate relationship between the campus and the community, and the neighborhood wasn't feeling very loving when Hopkins unveiled a plan to build a parking garage and thirteen-story tower to house the university bookstore, a bank, a post office and some retail business on the marine hospital parking lot. The Remington Improvement Association was so outraged about being left out of the decision-making process that they considered hiring a lawyer to help fight it. This wasn't the first time the neighborhood felt snubbed by the university. In the early 1960s, neighborhood leaders banded together to oppose a Hopkins proposal to buy 150 acres of parkland on both sides of Stony Run. In a compromise, Hopkins got a 30-acre strip, which today is the site of the Space Telescope. In 1985, the community loudly protested the school's leveling a portion of Wyman Park for use as an athletic field. The office tower was the final affront, and the community wasn't going to stand for it. The university proposed scaling back the project by eliminating the tower, but Remington responded that any retail would violate zoning laws, and the project was totally shelved. The university did, however, house all its loud and unsightly landscaping and auto repair facilities in its buildings facing Remington Avenue, so it may have had the last laugh.

Despite these community efforts, Remington's population continued to decline in the 1980s and 1990s. With low rates of employment and education, the freeze of social programs and the escalating crime rate, those with means to move away did. Nationwide drug epidemics struck Baltimore especially hard, and Remington was a niche that was targeted by drug dealers because of the easy access via the Twenty-eighth and Twenty-ninth Street bridges. They started doing business in the area, working from street corners and vacant homes. The crime rate skyrocketed as drug users burglarized homes and cars to help feed their habits, and drug sellers fought over territory. Homicides, almost unheard of in the area, resulted from the drug activity as well as from declining race relations and domestic violence. This was a citywide epidemic. By the mid-1980s, Baltimore was a city of contrasts, with its wildly successful Inner Harbor next to neighborhoods composed mostly of boarded-up houses. Public schools were in decline, but independent private schools grew stronger and diverse. Community health services were failing while medical advances at the Johns Hopkins institutions were on the rise.

Remington, however, knew how to take care of its own.

CHAPTER 7

# REDEFINING REMINGTON

## *Community Sustainability*

By 2000, the national housing market had begun to improve. After the country's large economic expansion in the 1990s, living in central cities became popular again after decades of urban decline and suburban expansion. Remington was becoming a viable location for investors and young, new residents seeking an affordable alternative to more expensive neighborhoods. With its decreased crime and low-cost housing, Remington was gaining popularity among students and staff at nearby educational institutions, as well as with the young professionals who preferred living near where they worked. In 2002, Remington still maintained a mantle of anonymity, until it gained nationwide attention for having been visited by the Beltway snipers, John Allen Muhammad and his teenage accomplice, Lee Boyd Malvo. After Muhammad and Malvo were arrested, it emerged that the pair had spent time in the Remington neighborhood, visiting the gas station on Sisson Street and the 7-Eleven on Twenty-eighth Street. They spent a night here sleeping in their 1990 Chevrolet Caprice. Luckily, the pair never released their fury on any Remingtonians, but the incident still gets discussed every time someone goes to that 7-Eleven.

In spite of this fleeting notoriety, the neighborhood was usually overlooked by people relocating to Baltimore City. True, commuters were aware that the Twenty-eighth and Twenty-ninth Street bridges transported them through unfamiliar territory, but the quick egress and ingress from these bridges did not allow proper attention to be paid by these travelers. Little did they realize that, by living in Remington, they could have easier-access corridors to and from the Jones Falls Expressway or that they could walk or shuttle to Pennsylvania Station and catch a train to work outside of Baltimore City.

Because it evolved from the settlement of the working-underclass, the neighborhood has been able to maintain its tradition of moderate density, pedestrian-scaled mobility and mixed uses. Residents view Remington's character as similar to a village, albeit within a larger urban context. The proximity of residences to commercial and industrial property and land demonstrates how closely tied the workers were to their places of employment.

In 2007, the Greater Remington Improvement Association (GRIA) was founded by community members who embarked on neighborhood beautification efforts, tree planting, community cleanup projects, community gardens and working with local businesses. The cost of living in Remington has been helped by numerous incentive programs for homebuyers, including Live Near Your Work grants and Healthy Neighborhoods loans, which GRIA actively promotes to current and new residents.

The demographics of Remington were remarkably changed when the dust had settled after the subprime mortgage crisis in 2008. Young professionals initially looking for starter homes to invest in had found Remington affordable and accessible to the rest of Baltimore City. The 2010 census provided proof of the neighborhood's increasing popularity as the population rose for the first time in over eighty years. Between 2000 and 2012, one hundred houses had become owner occupied, abandoned houses had decreased by almost 12 percent and the median age was between twenty-five and thirty-five. The big surprise, however, was the change in perception. New homeowners were no longer interested in "moving up the hill"; they liked it here, and they were determined to make their community the perfect place to live. So they needed a plan.

As demonstrated in earlier chapters, Remington grew rather haphazardly without a land use strategy. The railroad ran in people's backyards, utility companies sat squat in the center of row homes and light industrial inserted itself between neighbors. What was needed was a plan that would benefit all community investors. Beginning in 2008, the community, with leadership from the GRIA, sought technical assistance to develop a master plan that would address community needs. From mid-2008 to early 2009, the community worked with the Neighborhood Design Center (NDC) to begin the process of researching neighborhood history, creating a master plan steering committee and examining community plans from nearby communities. In March 2009, the master plan steering committee worked with community leaders to discuss what residents liked about Remington and to discuss opportunities to improve the neighborhood. Working along with the NDC, further opportunities for community engagement took place through the summer of 2009 to learn about the neighborhood's challenges and residents' ideas for its future. In September 2009, the master plan steering committee and NDC began holding monthly planning discussion sessions to discuss the community feedback gathered. While many residents were unaware of these sessions, vested parties such as businesses, local nonprofits, faith-based organizations, elected officials and GRIA members did attend. The sessions informed all of these interest groups of resident concerns and desires, made requests for further new ideas and put forth potential plan goals and recommendations. At the conclusion of the sessions, the master plan steering committee began to develop the master plan document. Further technical assistance was sought from the Greater Homewood Community Corporation and Johns Hopkins University for plan development. The plan presents a multi-year effort by the vested interest groups to put forth a vision for Remington to the year 2023, concentrating on several key elements: residential and commercial development, open space, mobility and public safety. A portion of the following contains extracts from that plan.

# RESIDENTIAL

One of Remington's greatest assets is the community's residential areas. Overall, the housing stock is well maintained and is generally affordable, supporting a mixed-income population. The community's residents believe this asset contributes to a sense of livability and are interested in preserving the housing stock in order to preserve and enhance the stability, affordability and character of the community for current and future residents.

Most homes in Remington are two- and three-story row houses with brick or Formstone fronts developed prior to 1939. While there are entire blocks of homes consisting of one architectural style, some row homes feature decorative marble or stained glass and house fronts that may be flat, swelled or bowed. Three-story homes tend to be clustered, and there are several duplex homes near Wyman Park. Multifamily housing stock includes Cresmont Lofts, a mid-rise apartment building built in 2004, and Miller's Court, a mixed-use apartment community that is housed in a former industrial building readapted for multifamily housing in 2009. Just outside the neighborhood's northeast boundary, Wyman House, a high-rise apartment building, provides low-income housing for senior citizens.

The planning committee determined that Remington's long-term success is ultimately dependent on trends occurring not just in the immediate vicinity but throughout Baltimore and in other large cities in the United States as well. Baltimore's population has been declining for over sixty years, but there are signs that it is stabilizing. Large swaths of the city that were once emptying out have been revitalized as new residents have moved in, renovating homes and rejuvenating tired commercial districts and parks.

According to 2010 U.S. Census data, approximately 14 percent of Remington's housing was not owner-occupied, an almost 2 percent decline since the 2000 census. In addition to detracting from the overall neighborhood character, residents have expressed that vacant properties are a draw for squatters and illegal activity, as well as potential health and safety hazards. It is possible that some of the vacant structures have deteriorated to a poor enough state that the structures may need to be demolished, making way for new or infill development. Several city and nonprofit programs had aided in the reduction of vacant housing, such as Vacants-to-Value that uses a receivership strategy to obtain vacant properties, and Healthy Neighborhoods, a program that helps people improve properties by offering low-interest loans and grants to buy, refinance and renovate their homes.

To continue to sustain Remington's socioeconomic diversity, community organizations and leaders urge current residents to take advantage of homestead tax credits and other city-based incentives for homeowners. These organizations also maintain that it is vital that the neighborhood continue to move forward with stability and livability efforts in order to serve its current population, particularly its at-risk residents. To this end, community organizations such as the Greater Remington Improvement Association, Remington Neighborhood Alliance and the Greater Homewood Community Corporation work hard to inform homeowners on the process of property tax assessment appeals and how to get assistance with renovations, as well as provide information about Healthy Neighborhood initiatives and programs that help to alleviate utility costs.

There are several opportunities for new and different-style housing. Because of the large amount of vacant commercial and industrial buildings and other vacant or underutilized properties, conversion to multi-use, mixed residential/commercial properties became one possibility for development. Of course, all new development in Remington would have to be within the Baltimore City zoning and housing code laws, and that may affect more venturous housing solutions.

## COMMERCIAL AND INDUSTRIAL

Over eighty businesses are located in Remington. The great majority are service providers whose clients are local, national and even international. A few retailers and food and beverage establishments cater to both Remington residents and surrounding neighborhoods. A few businesses have capitalized on the neighborhood's quirky character to market themselves to a citywide and regional audience. Charm City Cakes on Remington Avenue developed and hosted the Food Network's *Ace of Cakes*, one of that network's highest-rated shows. Except for the lower Howard Street corridor, small businesses and light industrial enterprises are scattered throughout Remington.

One of the more controversial development plans occurred in 2010 when Wal-Mart and Lowe's announced plans to open a retail shopping center on vacant property owned by Anderson Automotive. The city's oldest dealership, at Howard and Twenty-fifth Streets since 1955, was once known as Bill Mortimer's Anderson Olds and over the years added Chevrolet, Buick, Pontiac, GMC Truck, Hummer, Saab and Honda to its offerings. But the automotive industry had a severe downturn. The current owner of Anderson Automotive, Bruce Mortimer, received notice from GM that his Howard Street location franchise wasn't going to be renewed, so he decided to sell the portion of his property that housed GM vehicles to a developer that planned to invest tens of millions of dollars in the project that was to bring in hundreds of jobs to the neighborhood. The property was located on the west side of Howard Street, making it Remington territory, but the dealership itself straddles both sides of Howard Street for a couple blocks, so the Charles Village people believed they had an interest in the development also.

Developer Rick Walker unveiled his plans to build the complex, which, in addition to the home improvement store and retailer, would include thirty-two thousand square feet of specialty shops and up to sixty apartments. Walker, chief executive of Walker Developments Inc., had already obtained commitments from Lowe's and Wal-Mart, as well as financial backing, when he met with community association leaders. He thought his plans would go over well since that portion of the Howard Street corridor was no more than a dumping ground for car dealers and auto-related businesses. A majority of Remingtonians were excited by the prospect. No longer would they have to go to the suburbs to shop; they could now walk to major retail stores; and, with the economy having hit the neighborhood so hard, employment opportunities increased interest in the project. But there were also naysayers.

Even before "Andersonville," many auto dealers and repair shops could be found in this area of Howard and Twenty-fifth Streets. Notice the American Can Company in the background. *Courtesy of Betsy Childs.*

Differences over the project revealed a rift between rival community organizations and their competing visions for the up-and-coming neighborhood. The Remington Neighborhood Alliance and the Greater Remington Improvement Association shared their concerns regarding the traffic a new shopping center would incur, but they differed in their approach to dealing with the developers. In addition, a merchants' association was totally against the project, saying that the neighborhood needed more small businesses. Remingtonians began choosing sides and gearing up for a battle.

For over a decade, the Remington Neighborhood Alliance, headed by the wife-and-husband team of Joan Floyd and Doug Armstrong, advocated passionately for maintaining the community's character, while the newer Greater Remington Improvement Association focused on encouraging strategic development and preserving the neighborhood's character. It would not be the first time community groups were at loggerheads over Remington development.

The Alliance began in 2000, after the owner of Papermoon Diner, Un Kim, presented her plans for a restaurant and nightclub called Inferno to the community associations. Kim had acquired a $200,000 parcel behind her diner. The property housed a bunch of ramshackle garages and an alley that led to the 2800 block of Cresmont Avenue. The proposed nightclub would have live music, a fusion cuisine restaurant and a parking lot for both the diner and club. She promised the community that the club's target clientele would be "high-end" professionals in their thirties and forties and that there wouldn't be any noise problems, but residents were more concerned about drunken patrons and the increase in drug activity.

In an effort to promote her plans, Kim met with the newly formed Remington Neighborhood Alliance, bringing with her Alexander Ferranti, a family therapist, and Alfred W. Barry III, a planning consultant, to make her case during what turned out to be a very contentious meeting. Remington residents and Kim failed to resolve their differences over the proposed restaurant/lounge. Kim had offered to discard the name "Inferno" and plans for live music, but the Remington Neighborhood Alliance was more focused on the liquor license—and the fact that, despite her successful diner, Kim didn't live in Remington. Joan Floyd flatly told her, "If you need a liquor license, you need to come to this community." The Alliance members said they could mobilize enough neighbors to thwart a liquor license because a number of opponents lived within two hundred feet of the proposed restaurant. If more than half of the nearest neighbors oppose a license, state law requires the city liquor board to deny it. Kim was forced to abandon the project when the Board of Estimates—which includes the mayor, comptroller and city council president—refused to approve a state loan.

The site is now the location of the Cresmont Lofts, which was built in 2004, the same year Joan Floyd ran as an independent for city council, a fight Floyd failed to win.

When it came to the 25th Street Station project, the Remington Neighborhood Alliance and Floyd were prepared. She had studied the city's zoning code so thoroughly that she became a consultant for lawyers on zoning issues. However, the newer community association, GRIA, had built up a relationship with Remington that Floyd's group lacked. They had been busy organizing block parties, art classes, mural paintings and Halloween events. Members banded together to cut down invasive plants along Wyman Park, plant blueberry bushes by a 7-Eleven store and help set up a community garden on an empty lot on Fox Street. They were visible throughout the Greater Remington neighborhood and drew a large membership. The 25th

In an effort to reduce the tagging and graffiti on exposed surfaces, many community projects engaged artistic youths to participate in mural projects that were approved by both the city government and the buildings' owners. *Author's collection.*

Street Station project made the differences between the two community organizations very apparent.

Neither Remington community association was against the development project—which appeared to have the backing of many residents who were tired of driving to Dundalk or taking the light rail to Timonium to shop at Wal-Mart. Joan Floyd and the Remington Neighborhood Alliance actively focused on how the changes in zoning and development would impact Remington and its environment. Close attention was paid to the proper and timely filing of legal documents and impact studies. While keeping a close eye on the progress of this development, GRIA's concerns focused more on how the project would be beneficial to residents of Remington in terms of employment and convenience. A third organization, however, was spearheading the campaign against the involvement of Wal-Mart. Benn Ray, one-time president of the Hampden Merchants' Association and a Remington resident formed an organization called Bmore Local. This organization held a rally in front of city hall to protest the Wal-Mart store (though it seems nobody had a problem with Lowe's). Ray, the owner of Atomic Books in Hampden, believed small businesses presented better support for the neighborhood. An online petition drive called "No Wal-Mart in Remington" was created in February 2010. In support of Ray's efforts, John Waters, the grand master of Baltimore's quirkiness, spoke out against the Wal-Mart, warning that it would kill Remington's potential as a "hipster neighborhood." If three organizations with different viewpoints weren't enough, representatives from other neighborhoods containing or adjacent to the parcel—Charles Village and Old Goucher—also began meeting with the developers on traffic issues, further delaying the project.

Zoning legislation for 25th Street Station finally passed the city council in late 2010 after a long battle. The appeal of the legislation had been turned down at every level of the state's judiciary. Then Lowe's announced that it planned to close twenty underperforming stores in fifteen states as well as cut the number of new store openings in half during 2011. Included among those new stores planned but not going forward was the Remington site, which Lowe's was able to scrap under the conditions of its contract.

WV Urban Developments LLC (a corporation formed for this project by developer Rick Walker), said the Remington project would move ahead without Lowe's and still planned to redevelop the current site of Anderson Automotive with apartments as well as a Wal-Mart and other shops. Wal-Mart still planned to open a store at the project, but those plans hit another snag when Benn Ray and Brendan Coyne, who both live about four-tenths of a mile from the development site, filed suits that challenged the city-approved zoning change. They alleged that the project would have a negative effect on the neighborhood, depress local wages and make the streets more dangerous because of increased traffic flow. They complained that existing commercial establishments would close because of competition from the mega-retailer. Both suits were dismissed in Baltimore Circuit Court when it was decided the complainants failed to show that any of these local businesses would be adversely affected by the development and decreed the complainants did not live close enough for the traffic argument to be legally satisfactory. Also, an argument by Coyne that the development would decrease the value of his property was thrown out because he did not present the court with supporting expert evidence. The plaintiffs appealed their case to the Maryland Court of Special Appeals. This court released its unanimous opinion that Ray and Coyne were not eligible to appeal the Baltimore City Council's decision to grant the zoning approval for the project as they did not live close enough to the site to file such an appeal.

After the appeal had come to an end, the developer applied for the appropriate permits from Baltimore City and contracted to purchase the land from Bruce Mortimer, president of Anderson Automotive Group. Mortimer, however, had his own bone to pick with the project. He terminated the sale of the property and filed legal action against the developer, throwing into doubt the future of the much-debated project. Mortimer asked a Baltimore circuit judge to declare the sale legally terminated. In a complaint for declaratory judgment, Mortimer's company, Twenty Fifth Street LLC, contended that its sale agreements with the developer were effectively terminated in October 2012 when it missed its September 30, 2012 deadline to complete a purchase agreement with Wal-Mart Real Estate Business Trust, in which Wal-Mart would commit to purchasing a portion of the properties on the site. As of May 2013, further delays were possible as people in the neighborhoods surrounding the site continue to oppose its redevelopment. In addition, an overhaul of the city's zoning code is going through Planning Commission hearings and will soon be before the city council by the summer of 2013. That legislation might provide an opportunity to keep fighting 25th Street Station's construction. For now, it doesn't look like Remington will ever get a multi-use retailer development of the size planned for 25th Street Station. Stay tuned!

Luckily, the historical Baltimore pattern of corner stores on residential blocks has survived in the neighborhood, and they provide residents with basic staples, although many historical corner stores are no longer used in a commercial capacity. Other businesses have evolved along the more major streets and wherever permitted by zoning. There are significant areas of commercial property, with rows of houses sandwiched between. In addition to those operational businesses, there are several dozen spaces throughout Remington that are currently shuttered businesses or places where businesses have operated in the past, such as the above-mentioned corner stores. Numerous Remington residents operate businesses from their homes. Since these types of operations exist within private homes, devoid of signage or advertising, they are difficult to count. The community is still seeking to redevelop commercial enterprise within the neighborhood and will continue to monitor existing commercial, industrial and institutional business to ensure that the business owners recognize that they are located in a mixed use area and will develop and maintain their properties in a manner so that their particular uses are compatible with residential activities.

# OPEN SPACE

Open spaces are essential resources for the Remington neighborhood. Open spaces are those places that can be experienced by all community members: parks, community gardens, playgrounds and recreational facilities as well as private front yards and alleys. Open spaces serve as valuable assets that contribute to community character, enhance the infrastructure and provide places for relaxation and exercise. As the neighborhood continues to grow and change, steps can be taken to protect and preserve existing open spaces, identify opportunities for new ones, and ensure that these open spaces are accessible by community members. As we have seen, Wyman Park has two major elements that are regularly utilized by community members: the parkland itself and the Stony Run Trail. A newly formed volunteer-based organization named the Friends of Stony Run that initiates stream cleanups and programs to improve the health of the stream valley recently received a $600,000 grant to develop and maintain a continuous walking path from the Jones Falls Trail to north Baltimore along the original Ma & Pa Railroad line. Two ball fields have been resurrected on the park's south side, and the park also includes the GreenMount School, which has its own playfield.

Pocket parks and playgrounds exist throughout the community. At the corner of Thirtieth Street and Miles Avenue lies a small extension of Wyman Park. This pocket park includes a playground and a small, grassy green space. A small pocket park at Twenty-eighth Street and Fox Street contains four benches situated around an oval-shaped concrete play area. At Twenty-seventh Street and Miles Avenue, there is a vacant lot surrounded by a chain-link fence and covered with wood chips. It is accessible via a gate. The wall of the adjacent house is painted with an iconic "Remington" mural, depicted on this book's cover. This pocket park currently receives little use, and the children in the area are desperate for a more accessible and better-equipped space to play. Currently, children are playing ball in the streets. Little Little Italy has a small playground at the corner of Fawcett Street and Hampden Avenue. Some neighborhood children travel outside community boundaries to access the playground at Margaret Brent School that some Remington children attend. It contains playground equipment and a basketball court. The school and neighborhood are currently working on redesigning and rebuilding this important outdoor community space.

One aspect of sustainability the neighborhood has enthusiastically embraced is community gardens and orchards. Remington's Village Green is located on Fox Street, midway between Twenty-eighth and Twenty-ninth Streets. This roughly five-thousand-square-foot community garden was spearheaded in 2007 by Bill Skeen. Beth Barbush and Eric Imhof, original founding members of GRIA, and Moira Fratantuono oversaw the painting of murals on the buildings surrounding the garden. Participating gardeners grow a variety of produce during the summer months. Recent efforts have been made to establish other community gardens in the neighborhood. Vacant row house lots at the corner of Twenty-sixth Street and Miles Avenue were razed, and the land is now available for community planting. In 2009, residents of the community planted clusters of fruit trees throughout Remington. Tree types include peaches, plums, pears, pawpaws, apples, cherries and figs. The largest cluster is located at Twenty-ninth Street and Sisson Street and is known as the Remington Community Orchard. Other fruit trees are located on the 2700 block of Remington Avenue and the 500 block of Twenty-seventh Street. A half-acre lot on the corner of Twenty-seventh Street and Sisson Street. was purchased by Baltimore City in 2011 with the intention of creating a community space. Shortly thereafter, the community began planning how to use this land for the benefit of Remington residents. It is currently the garden space overseen by Bill Cunningham, but with community support, it could easily be shared as a playground.

Sidewalks are public spaces utilized by most Remington residents on a daily basis. They are used not just for mobility but also for socializing with neighbors and as areas for placing potted plants and greenery. Planting strips are the areas located between the sidewalk and street. They are usually less than ten feet in width and are present throughout Remington. Despite usually being in the public right-of-way, city regulations require that private property owners maintain these spaces. The maintenance and care of sidewalks and planting strips usually is an obvious indicator of how invested residents are in their community: well-maintained, weed-free sidewalks and planting strips with trees and shrubs show that residents care about the appearance of their block.

One notable neighborhood-wide effort to beautify Remington's planting strips was the placing of several dozen blue-painted wooden boxes in 2006. New shrubs and trees were planted inside the boxes. Although some remain, many of the boxes have since been removed due to lack of both maintenance and aesthetic value. Private front yards exist mostly in North Remington and are, for the most part, carefully maintained. Home ownership is a key factor in maintenance as temporary residents, such as college students and renters, are not always cognizant of the need to preserve appearances.

Alleys have traditionally been used for service purposes. Before modern technological infrastructure arrived in Baltimore, alleys were used to deliver materials used for heating and cooking. Currently, alleys are mostly used for the collection of trash and recyclables, but they also serve as play areas for Remington children. Their location in the rear of houses and primary function as service corridors often leads to their reputation as forgettable, repugnant spaces. In addition, lawbreakers often use alleys as places to take refuge or conduct illegal activities, causing alleys to become public safety liabilities. Neighborhoods in other parts of Baltimore have attempted to reclaim alleys as usable space. One of the most notable efforts is alley gating, where only the residents and sanitation workers have access to the right-of-way. As most Remingtonians are used to using alleys as shortcuts, any deterrents, such as gating, may face controversy.

Increasing the tree canopy has been promoted by the city's Tree Baltimore Urban Forestry Management Plan, which calls for doubling tree canopy over next thirty years. Increasing the number of trees in Remington can help to improve air and water quality, provide shade, beautify the streetscape and provide wildlife habitat. Remington has a number of blocks where shade trees enhance the living and pedestrian environment, including portions of Twenty-seventh Street, Wyman Parkway, Wyman Park Drive, Remington Avenue, Cresmont Avenue and Huntingdon Avenue. Realizing the potential to add more shade trees in Remington, residents, in partnership with the Parks and People Foundation, have engaged in an ongoing tree survey to identify distressed and decaying trees and identified areas for additional street tree plantings.

As we saw on our magical history tour, Remington developed from worker housing built close to places of employment. The neighborhood continued to develop as streetcar lines were added to the infrastructure. While streetcars are no long in existence, other forms of mobility have been introduced. The neighborhood's small scale still encourages walking, just like a century ago, but the predominance of cars and buses has caused major changes in Remington's appearance and function.

The primary form of point-to-point transportation within the neighborhood is walking. Remington's compact size, closeness of houses, proximity to neighborhood businesses and plentiful sidewalks provide community members with numerous opportunities for walking. There are approximately eleven miles of sidewalks within Remington, and most streets have sidewalks on both sides. According to the website Walkscore. com, which scores neighborhoods on accessibility to goods and services,

Remington currently has a walk score of eighty-seven, well above the city average of sixty-four. It is the twenty-seventh "most walkable" neighborhood in Baltimore. Approximately 19 percent of Remingtonians walk to work. Some residents utilize bicycles to reach points within the neighborhood and surrounding areas, and city-wide, bicycling is a popular option for commuting to work. Ownership and maintenance costs are much lower than those associated with owning a car, and bikes are much easier to store. Approximately 7 percent of Remington residents ride bicycles to work, but there are few bicycle amenities currently available. There is one signed bike route with "sharrows" along Wyman Parkway on the neighborhood's northern edge; this route connects with the Jones Falls Trail, just to the west. A few Remington businesses and community centers have installed designated bike parking. In 2011, several blocks of Huntingdon Avenue were chosen to be reconfigured for allowance of bike lanes.

Remington is currently served by two Maryland Transit Authority (MTA) bus routes. The #98 bus takes a circular route that connects Remington with Hampden and the Woodberry light rail stop. The #27 bus runs between Reisterstown Plaza in northwest Baltimore and Port Covington in South Baltimore. It provides access to neighborhoods such as Mount Washington, Roland Park, Hampden, Mount Vernon, downtown and Federal Hill. There are a total of nineteen bus stops in the neighborhood. According to the 2010 census, 23 percent of the neighborhood uses public transportation to commute to work.

Other public transit options are within walking distance. MTA buses run on the three nearest north–south streets in Charles Village. The #11 bus runs on Maryland Avenue and Charles Street, connecting suburban Towson with downtown, Fells Point and Canton. The #3 and #61 routes travel on Saint Paul and Charles Streets. The #3 bus connects Northeast Baltimore with downtown, while the #61 runs bus on a limited basis between the city center and the Roland Park area. The #13 bus, which runs on North Avenue, connects Remington to Walbrook in West Baltimore and large portions of East Baltimore, including Highlandtown, Fells Point, Canton and the Johns Hopkins medical campus. Baltimore's Light Rail travels to major transportation hubs like the Baltimore-Washington International Airport, Pennsylvania Station and Camden Station. It connects the city to suburban areas to the north and south. The nearest MTA Light Rail stop to Remington is at North Avenue, a little less than one mile from the center of the neighborhood and about a fifteen-minute walk. The Hampden Shuttle

Bug, MTA route #98, offers service directly to the Woodberry Light Rail station, which is two miles away from the center of Remington. Another major local transit system is the Metro Subway. The nearest station is at State Center, about a mile and a half away from Remington and is accessible on the #27 bus route. The subway currently connects Owing Mills Mall in Baltimore County to the Johns Hopkins Hospital in east Baltimore.

Pennsylvania Station is the closest major rail station, which is served by MARC commuter trains and Amtrak. Many Remington residents currently use MARC service to commute to jobs in the Washington, D.C. area. Bolt Bus, a long-distance bus company, currently stops in the Station North area, a fifteen-minute walk from central Remington. Bolt Bus offers direct service to New York City and Newark, New Jersey

The most obvious form of transportation through Remington is private and commercial automobiles. Remington's street network totals about seven miles and includes sixteen traffic signals. Only six of these signals are within Remington proper; the other ten are shared with adjacent neighborhoods. Among residents surveyed in 2010, 42 percent reported commuting to work by driving alone, while 9 percent carpooled. Approximately 87 percent of Remington households have access to at least one car.

Automobile travel into Baltimore City was greatly improved by the Interstate Highway program in the 1950s, and the Jones Falls Expressway (JFX) was the result of this program, completed in the early 1960s. The JFX included a new interchange, Exit 7, which required the building of the Twenty-eighth Street bridge. Today, eastbound Twenty-eighth Street and westbound Twenty-ninth Street are one-way, multi-lane thoroughfares that carry an enormous volume of traffic on and off the JFX. The great majority of people driving on these streets are not from the neighborhood, and many do not even live in Baltimore City. Because there are few traffic lights on these streets, traffic often moves at speeds much higher than the legal limit. Howard Street, the main commercial street on the east side of Remington and Sisson Streets and the main thoroughfare on the neighborhood's western edge, carries substantial volumes of commercial traffic. Other primary streets include Huntingdon Avenue and Remington Avenue, which both contain the highest concentrations of businesses in the Greater Remington area. These streets are also heavily residential as well. Both streets connect to major arteries in adjacent neighborhoods.

# Public Safety

As mentioned earlier, Remington is a neighborhood with significant community cohesion and involvement. However, crime and sanitation issues impact neighborhood safety. Over the past decade, crime—particularly property crimes and illegal drug activity—has been of great concern to residents. Vacant buildings located throughout Remington exacerbate crime issues in the community, providing hidden or partially hidden spaces for illegal activity to take place. To discourage criminal activity, the Remington community associations and residents continuously liaise with the Northern District Baltimore City Police Department, sharing concerns regarding suspicious activity observed in the community.

Overall, Remington's crime rate is slightly higher than the city's average, but lower than many surrounding neighborhoods. Based on public data, most crime is centered in the Greater Remington area, with the 2600 block of Miles Avenue being the worst for violent crime and the 200 block of West Twenty-sixth Street the worst for property crime.

Both violent crime and property crime have declined dramatically from ninety-six reported incidences in 2007 to thirty-two reported incidences in 2012. The great majority of blocks in Remington have had little or no violent crime in recent years. For example, the 2900 block of Miles Avenue had seven violent crimes between 2007 and 2009, but has not experienced a single incident since. Some blocks have higher numbers largely because of one or two businesses that are repeatedly targeted. For example, the 7-Eleven convenience store on Twenty-eighth Street was robbed on eleven different occasions over six years, which represents over half the crimes on that block. Because the store is on a major thoroughfare, most of the criminals are not residents of the Remington neighborhood. Blocks that rarely experience violent crime, such as those north of Twenty-ninth Street, sometimes have property crime. In addition, the neighborhood's convenience stores often deal with petty theft incidents, which lead to higher property crime rates. Like violent crime, property crime appears to also be on the decline, based on the reported data.

# SANITATION

Maintaining cleanliness in outdoor areas, controlling trash, preventing rat and rodent infiltration, reducing water pollution, recycling and curtailing illegal dumping activities are important. City sanitation workers can also be guilty of harming the neighborhood's cleanliness. On trash and recycling pickup days, employees don't always do a complete job, and alleys and streets are often strewn with items that Public Works employees missed or neglected to collect. Many residents and visitors are guilty of poor sanitation habits that cause public health and environmental concerns. Some of these actions include: failing to use lids on trash cans, which allows trash to be blown away by the wind and provides rats with a steady food supply; not recycling, which increases the likelihood of wind-blown trash and results in more landfill space being used; littering, which feeds rats and rodents, clogs storm drains and creates an unsightly appearance; and pouring hazardous chemicals and substances on the street, which pollutes waterways like Stony Run, the Jones Falls and Chesapeake Bay. A major topic of concern for Remingtonians is the dumping of large quantities of bulk trash along property that is owned and supposedly maintained by the CSX railroad. The community associations are working with CSX to combat this illegal dumping and drafting a proposal for continued maintenance. Community leaders hold neighborhood-wide events to raise awareness about trash and sanitation in Remington. Residents have been given free trash cans and recycling bins to encourage their use. Regular cleanup events are held throughout the year, giving residents numerous opportunities to contribute to a cleaner community. Baltimore City has multiple bulk-trash days each year where residents can dispose of large items, and of course, Remington still has the Sisson Street collection center.

# AFTERWORD

So how are we doing? You've seen Remington past, present and future and the residential commitment to redefine and sustain the neighborhood. At this writing, the 25th Street Station is still struggling to become a reality. In the meantime, the corner of Twenty-eighth Street and Remington Avenue has been bought by a developer who is planning a mini-mall, if the proper zoning exists. Across the street, the "sniper" 7-Eleven is transferring ownership, and a couple blocks down on Howard Street will be the site of the Single Carrot Theater and Woodberry Kitchen, an organic restaurant/butcher shop. The *Remington Community Newsletter*, edited by Betsy Childs, is hand-delivered to every household in the neighborhood. We now have several websites and Facebook pages dedicated to Remington. Things are moving quite fast, and these past five years have been exciting ones for a diverse yet cohesive neighborhood intent on remaining that way. Baltimore City is finally taking some notice of our little community, and new neighbors are flowing in, but we still have a long way to go. Hopefully, this publication will allow those new to the area, as well as our friends and neighbors, to realize how important our village is to the history and the future of Baltimore and incite them to join those of us who have firmly put down our roots here. As a young man once said, "I'll never leave!"

# SELECTED BIBLIOGRAPHY

America's Historical Newspapers. http://infoweb.newsbank.com.

Barnes, Robert W. *Colonial Families of Maryland: Bound and Determined to Succeed.* Baltimore: Genealogical Publishing Co., 2007.

Brooks, Neal A., and Eric G. Rockel. *A History of Baltimore County.* Towson, MD: Friends of the Towson Library Inc., 1979.

Brugger, Robert J. *Maryland, A Middle Temperament: 1634–1980.* Baltimore: Johns Hopkins University Press, 1988.

Chapelle, Suzanne Ellery Greene. *Baltimore: An Illustrated History.* Sun Valley, CA: American Historical Press, 2000.

Citizens Planning and Housing Association. *Beyond the White Marble Steps: A Look at Baltimore Neighborhoods.* Baltimore: Boarman Company, 1979.

Dilts, James D. *The Great Road: The Building of the Baltimore and Ohio, the Nation's First Railroad, 1828–1853.* Stanford, CA: Stanford University Press, 1993.

Hayward, Mary Ellen, and Charles Belfoure. *The Baltimore Rowhouse.* New York: Princeton Architectural Press, 1999.

Hollified, William. *Difficulties Made Easy.* Baltimore: Baltimore County Historical Society, 1978.

Kelly, Jacques. *Virtue and Vice, Poverty and Riches.* Baltimore: SS Philip and James Church, 1997.

LeWand, Karen, and D. Randall Beirne. *North Baltimore: From Estate to Development.* Baltimore: Department of Planning and the University of Baltimore, 1989.

Maryland Historical Society. War Records Division. *Maryland in World War II: Register of Service Personnel*. Baltimore: Maryland Historical Society, 1965.

Maryland State Archives. www.msa.maryland.gov.

————. Digital Image Retrieval System for Land Records in Maryland. www.mdlandrec.net.

Mayer, Brantz. *Baltimore: Past and Present*. Baltimore: Richardson & Bennett, 1871.

Mayre, William B. "Baltimore City Place Names: Stony Run, Its Plantations, Farms, Country Seats and Mills." *Maryland Historical Magazine* 58, no. 3 (September 1963): 211–32.

McGrain, John. *The Molinography of Maryland: A Tabulation of Mills, Furnaces, and Primitive Industries*. Towson, MD: John McGrain, 1976, rev. 2007.

Melosi, Martin V. "The Place of the City in Environmental History." *Environmental History Review* 17, no. 1 (Spring 1993): 1–23.

————. *The Sanitary City: Urban Infrastructure in America from Colonial Times to the Present (Creating the North American Landscape)*. Baltimore: Johns Hopkins University Press, 2000.

Olson, Sherry H. *Baltimore, the Building of an American City*. Expanded bicentennial ed. Baltimore: Johns Hopkins University Press, 1997.

Proquest Historical Newspapers. *Baltimore Sun (1837–1987)* http://search.proquest.com/hnpbaltimoresun.

Sattler, Eugene. *My Memories, My Century, My Life*. unpublished manuscript.

Scharf, J. Thomas. *The Chronicles of Baltimore: Being a Complete History of "Baltimore Town" and Baltimore City*. Baltimore: Turnbull Brothers, 1874.

Varle, Charles. *A Complete View of Baltimore*. Baltimore: Samuel Young, 1833.

# INDEX

**A**

ABC Row  41
Ace of Cakes  105
Action in Maturity  96
Al's Tavern  75
American Ice Company  72
Anderson Body Shop  79
Armstrong, Doug  106
Atkinson, James H.  32
Atomic Books  109

**B**

Babbitt, Dora  52
Baltimore and Ohio Railroad  38
Baltimore Glass Company  79
Baltimore Passenger Railway  47
Baltimore Streetcar Museum  38, 48, 92
Baltimore Water Company  18
Barbush, Beth  79
Baxley, John  29
Bay, James  20
Bay, Jane  20, 48, 81
Beefmaster's Restaurant  56
Beltway Sniper  101
Bethany United Evangelical Church  55
Birckhead, Solomon  23
Bolt Bus  115

Brouard, Kai  98
Brown, Thomas  72

**C**

Carroll, David  18
Carter, Henry R.  63
Cedar Avenue  48, 83
Cedar Avenue Bridge  48
Central Relief Committee of Baltimore  33
Charles Carroll of Carrollton  13
Charles Street  45
Charm City Cakes  105
Chilcote, William L.  45
Children's Hospital School  70
City Dairy Company  64, 74
Clarke, Mary Pat  57
Community School  56, 57
Community Survival Center  56
Consolidated Gas & Electric  43
Convalescent Home for Crippled Colored
        Children  69
Cooper, Thomas  29
Corky's Restaurant  71
Cox, Linda  97
Cresmont Avenue  95
Cresmont Lofts  103, 107
Crouch, Phil  78
CSX  41, 117

Culotta, Tom 55
Cunningham, Bill 75, 112
Curley, John 33

## D

Davis, George W. 29
DeLuca, Teresa 73
Detorie, Nicholas 73
Dieter, Nick 75
Druid Hill 46, 49

## E

Easter Parade 89
electric railway 41
Ellicott, John 29
Ellsberry, John 46
Elmo, Michangelo 73
Ensor, Joseph 13
Ensor's Run 20

## F

Falls Road 49
Falls Road tollgate 29
Falls Turnpike Road Company 29
Fawcett, Emmor 72
Fawcett Street 72
Floyd, Joan 107
Fox Street 107
Franciscan Sisters of Baltimore 53
Frank and Yetta's Jewish Deli 75

## G

Gambrill, Horatio N. 23
Garrett, Frances 13
Gibbons Guild 55
Gilpin, Bernard 15
Gilpin, Jim 78
Glen Edwards Avenue 41, 60, 72, 73
Goldberg's Hardware Store 76
Good Husbands' Row 41, 71
Greater Faith Baptist 96
Greater Homewood Community
    Corporation 57, 95, 103
Greater Remington Improvement
    Association 62, 102, 107

Great Fire of 1904 96
GreenMount School 97
Greenspring Avenue 70
Guardian Angel Church 52, 55, 57

## H

Haile, Nicholas 11
Haile's Addition 11, 13, 15
Haines, Nathan 72
Hampden Avenue 41, 78
Hampden Merchants' Association 108
Hanson, Jonathan 14
Hard Times Tavern 76
Harris, John 31
Hauntingdon 79
High's Dairy 74
Hollingsworth, Samuel 15
Hollingsworth's Dam 25
Hollingsworth's Mill 15, 17
Homewood Park 91
Howard Street 72, 105
Howard Street Bridge 45
Hudson, Thomas 57
Huntingdon Avenue 35, 57, 72
Huntingdon Avenue Bridge 45, 47
H. White Mill 18

## I

Inferno Nightclub 107

## J

Jackson and Lee monument 92
Jane Bay Hall 83
Jane Bay Home for Boys 20, 81
Jarman Pontiac 79
Jefferson Place 72
J.E. Greiner Company 46
Jenkins, Hugh 23
Jessop, Charles 29
Jessop, William 29
Johns Hopkins Colored Orphan Asylum 68
Johns Hopkins Community Physicians 68
Johns Hopkins Hospital 63
Johns Hopkins University 65, 83, 98, 103
Jones Falls 45, 64

Jones Falls Expressway  46, 102
Jones Falls Trail  111
Jones Falls Turnpike  27
Justice, Charles  35
Justice, Nelson  35

## K

Kavanagh, Hugh Ignatius  53
Kayo gas station  79
Keen Memorial Baptist Church  55, 84,
      95, 96
Keswick A.C  60
Keswick Avenue  48
Kim, Un  79, 107
King Iron Bridge Manufacturing
      Company  49
King Street  69
Kromer, George  50
Krout, Charles  38
Krout, Robert S.  37

## L

Larkins, William A.  64
Latrobe, Charles H.  48
Laurell Merchant Mill  23
Leggett, George  23, 29
Liberty Roofing Company  73
Liliendale  13
Litzinger, Charles E.  83
Long John's Pub  78
Lynch, Edward  29
Lynch, William  29

## M

Manion, Birdie Mae  86
Mankin, Henry  29
Ma & Pa  38, 47
Maryland and Pennsylvania Railroad  38
Maryland Construction Company  72
Mason, William  23
McDonogh School for Boys  83
Meet 27  56
Merryman's Lane  48
Meyers, William Patrick  56
Miller's Court  103

Mitchell's  89
Mooney, Agnes  35
Mooney, John  35
Mortimer, Bruce  110
Mount Royal  14
Mount Royal Avenue  89
Mount Royal Forge and Mill  15, 23, 31
Mount Royal Hill  35
Mount Vernon Mills  29, 30, 72, 73

## N

North Avenue  38
Northern Central Railroad  38
Northern Central Railroad Company  35
North Remington  81

## O

Oaks Athletic Association  60
Oak Street  72
Oak Street AME  55
Open House Coffee Shop  79

## P

Palmer, Dorothy  84
Palmer, Henry Harrison  83
Papermoon Diner  79, 107
Patapsco Lower Hundreds of Baltimore
      County  11
Peabody Heights Academy  53
Peddicord, Isaac H.  31
Pennington, Josias  15, 27
Pennsylvania Railroad  38
Pennsylvania Station  115
Phoebus, Tom  60, 74
Piney's Tavern  75
Potts & Callahan  46, 78, 96
Precipice Place  41
Preston, James H.  63

## R

Ray, Benn  108
Red Cross Gray Ladies  68
Remington A.C  58
Remington Avenue  41, 57, 65
Remington Avenue Bridge  50

Remington Community Orchard 112
Remington Groceries 78
Remington Improvement Association 95
Remington Juniors 60
Remington Neighborhood Alliance 62,
    104, 106, 107, 108
Remington, William 91
Riley, Frank 36
Robinson, Dan 79
Rock Merchant Mill 15, 18
Russell, Lefty 60

**S**

Sanitary Laundry and Dry Cleaning 75
Sattler, Eugene 87
Sattler, Joseph Bernard 86
Schedel, George 78
Schier, Carl F. 74
Schier, Oscar B. 74
Schier's Hygeia Dairy 74
Schultheis, John 72
Schwind, John G. 32, 33
Seed Ticks Plenty 13
Shirk, Henry 45
Shuttle Bug 115
Sisson, Hugh 72
Sisson Street 41, 74
Sisson Street Bridge 45, 71
Sisters of Mercy 53
Skeeter Scare of 1915 63
Smith, Winford 69
SS Philip and James Academy 53, 87
SS Philip and James Catholic Church 53
Stack, John 53
Stewart, James 29
Stony Run 11, 45, 47, 64, 71, 117
Stony Run Trail 111
Stony Works Cotton Factory 23
Sumwalt Pond 64, 65
Sun Cab 74
Sunderland, Florence E. 83
Swann Lake Railroad 20

**T**

Taggart, William 23
Thirty-third Street Bridge 50

Thornberry, Troy 85
Three Mile House 75
Timanus, Mayor E. Clay 18
T&T Food Market 78
Turner Place 72
Twenty-eighth Street Bridge 46
25th Street Station 107, 110
Twenty-ninth Street Bridge 45
Twenty-third Street 41
Tyson, Elisha 15, 23, 29

**U**

Union Electric Railway Company 47, 48
Union Mill 15, 23
United States Public Health Service 66
U.S. Marine Hospital 63, 65, 83

**V**

Vacants-to-Value 57, 104
Valenza, Andrea 75

**W**

Walker, Rick 105
Wal-Mart 108
Walpert, Allan N. 78
Walters, Ken 75
Western Maryland Dairy Company 74
Western Maryland Railroad 38
Williams, Caroline Barney 91
Woodberry Light Rail 115
Wrightson, William D. 64
Wyman and Remington memorial 93
Wyman House 104
Wyman Park 62, 71, 83, 103
Wyman Park Baseball 60
Wyman Park Dell 91
Wyman Park Drive 83
Wyman Park Multipurpose Center 96

# ABOUT THE AUTHOR

Kathleen C. Ambrose is a native of Baltimore with long ties to the Remington neighborhood. She purchased a home there while attaining her masters of liberal arts from the Johns Hopkins University and has been a Remingtonian for the past fifteen years. Always fascinated with local history, Ms. Ambrose serves on the boards of the Friends of Stony Run and the Baltimore City Historical Society. She is a member of the Maryland Historical Society, as well as the Historical Society of Baltimore County, and is often seen photographing throughout all sections of the neighborhood.